FOOD
FOR ALL
SEASONS

Scottish Food Promotion

FOOD
FOR ALL
SEASONS

The New Scottish Cooking

Introduced by Neil MacLean

MOUBRAY HOUSE PUBLISHING

FOOD FOR ALL SEASONS
The New Scottish Cooking
introduced by Neil MacLean
with Joanna Blythman, Kirsty Burrell,
Tess Darwin, Sandra Macpherson

Photographs:
Marius Alexander (pp 15, 17, 19, 40, 44, 47, 48, 54)
Alasdair Foster (pp 62, 65, 78/79, 82)
Stuart Hamilton (pp 24, 28, 31, 39, 65, 66, 77)
Douglas MacGregor (pp 6, 12, 43, 58, 61, 73)
Neil MacLean (pp 11, 12, 26, 27, 43, 61, 74, 81)
Louis Flood (p 13), Michael Siebert (p 21)
Watercolour illustrations: Maggie Smith
Botanical drawings: Mary Bates
Recipe section illustrations: Edna Whyte
Designed by Dorothy Steedman
Moubray House Publishing wishes to thank the following for help in
the production of this book:
Ariane Burgess, Damaris Fletcher, Claire Macdonald,
Paul Rogerson, Tessa Bennett Antiques,
Frâiche Delicatessen, Valvona & Crolla, Eliot Clark Flowers,
Dunedin Fruits & Vegetables, Budget Tiles & The Mill Shop, Aberfeldy

ISBN: 0948473 10 X
Published in Scotland in 1989
by Moubray House Publishing Ltd.
Tweeddale Court, 14 High Street,
Edinburgh EH1 1TE
Copyright Moubray House Publishing Ltd. 1989
Printed in Scotland by The Eagle Press, Blantyre
Typeset in-house in Garamond

British Library Cataloguing in Publication Data
Food for all Seasons: the new Scottish Cooking
1. Food: Scottish dishes
641.3'009411

FOOD FOR ALL SEASONS
CONTENTS

SCOTTISH FOOD FOR ALL SEASONS

Over the last decade cooks and chefs in Scotland have been exploring the hidden corners of their natural larder, and a new style of cooking has emerged which emphasises the value of Scottish ingredients gathered at their seasonal best. The public is catching on and there is interest and excitement about it everywhere you go. The contributors to *Food For All Seasons* reflect the new culinary art of Scotland as it makes itself felt in the growing and gathering of produce, in the best restaurants, whether simple or grand, at home and in our traditional recipes.

Begin with the land and the sea: the land mass of Scotland, its climate and the waters round its coasts combine to produce the best natural larder in the world. There are fields of grain, vegetable and fruit crops, grasslands for animals, woodlands of fungi, wild places rich with game and teeming seas and rivers. The sea is cold but tempered by a warmer drift in the west - perfect conditions for fish and shellfish of outstanding quality.

Then consider the people: those who trawl the deep sea fish, who dive for scallops, set lobster creels, tend oyster beds and mussels, smoke fat fillets of fish and lamb, venison and bacon, milk cows and goats and ewes for cheese, cultivate the land to grow acres of fruit and grain and root crops - the Scots who tend the natural larder.

Scotland has developed its fine natural larder over the centuries and its people have always been prepared to work the land and the sea. But it has only recently become celebrated for the skill of its best chefs and cooks, who have moved far beyond an ability to make simple dishes and warming soups like haggis and cock-a-leekie, which the rest of the world likes to think is its staple fare.

Now there is talk of a school of modern Scottish cooking. But the emphasis on natural taste and the attractive presentation of food which is not masked by foreign flavours, belongs to a movement which has

Award-winning chefs recognise the importance of using the natural larder at its seasonal best and happily don wellington boots to seek out organic vegetables, wild plants, mushrooms and the like. Charles Price is one, seen here on a visit to the well-manured field of an organic farm near Dumbarton with (clockwise from left): Andrew McCairn, waiter; goat tenders; organic farmer Echo Mackenzie; dairy products suppliers Jim and Karen Perrat; hotelier Chris Longden; butcher Drew Mackenzie with a sirloin of beef on the bone; Robert Morris, supplier of fish, game, poultry, fruit, vegetables and cheese; and (foreground) food writer Neil MacLean who helps to influence taste and set standards.
Local demand for top quality produce and awareness of international trends are transforming Scottish cooking. Outstanding cooks and chefs stress the importance of using the natural larder at its seasonal best and the vital part played by each link in the food chain: growers, producers, suppliers, chefs, cooks and the discerning customer

developed in kitchens all over the world. Top international chefs are united by a common purpose and willingness to explore and reflect their local and national resources. This is the vital ingredient which make the food of one region different from another. And the best Scottish chefs and cooks, who are in tune with the seasons and using local produce, are preparing what is recognisably Scottish food - but in a modern style.

Credit for the recent revolution in Scotland's culinary art, however, does not rest solely with the chefs or cooks. Their suppliers are playing a major part by listening to what the chefs want and by showing themselves willing both to develop new products and improve on the quality of existing lines. It is a measure of the widespread interest in Scotland's fine food that you can now buy exquisite baby cauliflowers from Grangemouth, flowering courgettes from Mallaig, oysters from Finstown in Orkney and ewe's milk cheese from Lanark.

What the chefs cannot buy locally they will often produce themselves. It is not unusual to find a polythene tunnel close to a hotel on the west coast providing shelter for the new season's vegetables. Or to look out of your hotel window one spring morning to see the cook feeding a cluster of ducks, or catch a glimpse of an award winning chef in wellington boots and muffler heading for a wooded glen in search of ceps and other wild mushrooms.

These people are leading from the front. Whereas in France there is a long history of gastronomy and a tradition of good food at home and in the smallest restaurants, in Scotland the message has still to percolate down from the best professional kitchens to the amateur cook. There is still some way to go, and the next stage involves improving supplies to the home. This is a two-way process, as Joanna Blythman points out in her articles on cheese, meat and fish in this book, and the public needs to encourage retailers to stock new lines, improve quality and divert some of the top quality produce from its well-worn path across to the Continent and into the home market.

The new awareness of the unexplored potential of the Scottish larder began in the early 1970s. At that time, many of the top professionals in Scotland trained in hotels owned by the former British Transport Hotels (BTH) group. This provided a good step-by-step training which took them through the basics of their trade, taught them how to work and set them on a path towards kitchens of their own. Many were influenced by two men in particular - Stewart Cameron and Paul Rogerson who worked together at the Gleneagles Hotel in Perthshire. Stewart Cameron from Dunblane was first sous chef in the great Chef Cottet's kitchen. After he left Gleneagles, he worked as head chef at the Station Hotel in Perth, the Central Hotel in Glasgow and the famous Turnberry Hotel near Ayr. He has been responsible for training many of Scotland's best young chefs who are now working in top restaurants throughout the world. But Stewart Cameron himself is first to agree that it was Chef Cottet's second sous chef at Gleneagles, Paul Rogerson, who really developed a new way with Scottish produce.

In 1972, Gleneagles Hotel closed for the winter after a long hard season, and, as usual, many of the chefs looked elsewhere for winter work. Paul Rogerson was offered the chance to teach some of the catering students at Inverness Technical College and it was in Inverness that he first realised that contemporary chefs were not making the most of Scottish produce. He wanted to encourage them to try a simpler style using fresh local supplies, traditional dishes with a lighter touch and to use some of the ideas of presentation that he had picked up when he worked in Germany.

At that stage it was still an embryonic idea, but shortly after he returned to Gleneagles, he was promoted to another of the BTH hotels at Kyle of Lochalsh. Now head chef, he was able to experiment and to develop his ideas further, inspired by the beauty of the local scenery and its wonderful produce. But, although he was able to serve special parties with his modern Scottish dishes from the kitchen on a plate, silver service was still the rule in the Kyle hotel and if he produced what became his hallmark, a piece of beef and a lamb cutlet with a duo of sauces, the front of house staff would frequently ruin the presentation by mixing the sauces.

It was only after he moved to the Station Hotel in Inverness, and after many battles against convention, that his ideas about modern cooking and plated service became accepted. While he was there he influenced younger Scottish chefs, like Charles Price, Peter Jackson, Bill Gibb, Michael Simpson and Ian MacDonald, who were later to become head chefs in Scottish hotels.

There was no going back for Paul, who took his modern Scottish menu and plated service to the Caledonian Hotel in Edinburgh. Even after a waiter dropped fifty of the hotel's best plates, the staff nobly continued plated service with the few plates left and a lot of washing up. Paul Rogerson's culinary art soon became the toast of the town. But half a decade later, he has chosen to train the next generation of chefs at the Jewel and Esk Valley College where he urges his pupils to respect the wealth of Scotland's larder. With BTH training no longer an option, however, it is now up to chefs like Jackson, Sangster and Price to take youngsters from Paul's tutelage, and from the other catering schools, and provide them with the experience they need to develop further.

But this book is not just about professionally trained chefs. The cooking of the best amateurs, often working in small family-run hotels and restaurants, has developed in tandem with that of the professionally trained chefs, and has been recognised and rewarded both by word of mouth and by food critics.

David Wilson, a native of Bishopriggs, finally won a coveted Michelin star in 1987 after years of cooking some of the best food in Scotland. He was a marketing executive in London when he decided that he wanted to run a restaurant. He spent a year gaining confidence and experience in kitchens in English restaurants, before he and his wife Patricia bought the old, run-down Peat Inn near St Andrews. At about the

Outstanding self-taught cooks:
Gunn Eriksen (opposite top) has the cooking equivalent of perfect pitch and Michelin star award winner David Wilson cooks some of the best food in the country which brings out the strong flavours of Scottish ingredients

time when Paul Rogerson was developing his own style in Kyle of Lochalsh, David Wilson was absorbing the new ideas of the French chef Michel Guérard and encouraging local producers to supply him with the best that Fife could offer.

Now his cooking reflects the area where he lives. He will not buy foreign produce if he can help it - even his rich dark truffles come from Scottish soil. He relishes the strong flavours of good Scottish ingredients, including those that might have seemed unfashionable: turnips (not the sweet baby vegetables, but the traditional Scottish neeps), offal (again traditionally Scottish) and Arbroath smokies. His philosophy is to bring out these flavours, perhaps with others added, but only to enhance, certainly not to overwhelm, and to present his dishes attractively.

While there are new and better ways to cook Scottish produce, these chefs know that other dishes are best left unaltered. With many game recipes, for example, we find that there are good pragmatic reasons for following the traditional approach. Certainly the choice is there and Sandra Macpherson, one of the contributors to *Food For All Seasons*, offers a valuable reminder of the traditional approach.

However many naturally Scottish ingredients have lost their place in our culinary repertoire. Modern chefs would do well to rediscover some of the wild food that is growing on the hillsides, in the hedgerows and by the sea. Tess Darwin, an ecologist who is making a detailed study of wild food, points the way in this book by describing how to find and use it, season by season.

One cook who has discovered the wild food around her is Gunn Eriksen. Gunn has the tasting equivalent of perfect pitch. She tries plants and seaweeds near her small hotel, and decides what will complement her evening menu. Dulse, ground elder, samphire, bittercress and hawthorn leaves - all have their place in her kitchen at Altnaharrie.

It comes as a surprise to learn that Gunn Eriksen became a professional cook by accident. She left her native Norway to travel the world - a journey that,

Paul Rogerson (top) trains the next generation of cooks and chefs at the Jewel and Esk Valley College; and, milk and honey from Jim and Karen Perrat, the father and daughter team which has built up a profitable dairy products business from the family's milk-round

in the end, only took her as far as Inverness. There she met Fred Brown who invited her back to his small hotel at Altnaharrie, beside Loch Broom.

Just before the beginning of the season a husband and wife team, who had agreed to take over the running of the hotel from Fred in 1980, changed their minds. Gunn went into the kitchen, put on her apron and found that she had two weeks to teach herself how to cook. Since then her cooking has proved a revelation to guests in her diningroom across the sea. Like David Wilson, she feels that self-taught cooks have an advantage over the professionally trained; they are freer to interpret the ingredients presented to them, unfettered by culinary convention.

However the common denominator shared by all the cooks, chefs and writers in this book, whatever their respective backgrounds, is a passion for Scottish food and an interest in promoting the best produce of our natural larder in season. Kirsty Burrell, for example, insists on using top quality produce, simply prepared, and likes to reflect seasonal celebrations in her family cooking. As anyone exploring the new culinary art of Scotland will discover, imagination is an important quality as is an unwillingness to accept inferior products imported from somewhere else. The hotels and restaurants selected here are places which reflect the recent revolution in Scottish food. The kitchens of the chefs and cooks, their recipes, the workplaces of the best suppliers, are not offered as altars at which to worship a new cuisine. *Food For All Seasons* is intended to be a practical source of delight and inspiration for readers who are fortunate enough to have access to the best natural larder in the world.

Neil Maclean

EDINBURGH, 1989

12

FOUR WRITERS : FOUR SEASONS

introduced by Fay Young

The contributors to Food for all Seasons are influencing the trasformation of Scottish eating habits. Food writer Neil MacLean's idea of heaven is a picnic in perfect weather from a hamper stuffed with seasonal produce

Neil MacLean's first job involving food was doling out stewed tea, jam sandwiches and Knorr soup to alcoholics in Glasgow's George Square. Now Glasgow's miles better; there is an upmarket wine bar on the soup-kitchen site selling quiche and 'Death by Chocolate' cake and the people living on hair spray have moved somewhere down and out.

The irony was not lost on the freelance food and travel writer visiting George Square recently. Neil MacLean's new job means eating with the other half in nouvelle and expensive places but, savouring a top class meal, he remembers exactly what packet soup tastes like and it certainly keeps him down to earth.

But that does not stop him enjoying the job which takes him to the best of hotels and restaurants in Scotland and throughout the rest of the world. He says he meets Glaswegians cooking and catering in all sorts of places, Kenya, St Lucia: 'I'm not sure whether they are running away from the old Glasgow or the new.'

Neil spikes his story with plenty of jokes and self-mockery. He dropped out of Scottish Literature studies at University into the Church of Scotland alcoholics programme because of his social conscience. Both parents were doctors which might or might not have had something to do with it. He was a dab hand at a 33-egg scramble, and Silverside for

Sunday lunch ('I must have ruined the programme's food budget'). Ready for a change, he dropped into freelance writing with regular work for Sunday newspapers and magazines. He has always enjoyed food and likes travelling for the differences and similarities it turns up. 'Standing in Grenada looking at a little hilly mound you think: that's just like Arisaig.' There are similarities in people too, and, at its best, food tastes different in foreign places.

There is a faint touch of evangelism in Neil's enthusiasm for the new Scottish excellence in food. He makes a point of passing on information in his articles, about the new Scottish cheeses, for example, particularly in restaurants offering a tired, predictable old cheese board. He praises the increasing number of restaurants offering only the very best Scottish ingredients cooked with skill and imagination. And he very much enjoys the lack of preciousness among the chefs and cooks who are more concerned with taste than appearance. 'There don't seem to be so many prima donna chefs in Scotland as elsewhere and success doesn't go to their heads; some of them have come from rough places you don't immediately associate with haute cuisine and they keep in touch with their roots.'

His main regret is that the public is not able to buy the excellent meat, fish and vegetables made available to the catering trade. 'We probably have to get away from the idea of looking for a bargain and be prepared to pay for the best. But you need a butcher you can talk to and you need one who knows how to cook.' However things are changing: who would have thought you could buy courgette flowers from Mallaig, guinea fowl and Gressingham duck in Arran, ewe's milk cheese north of Inverness and free-range bacon from Glentarkie?

Neil writes about these things, but does not cook much for himself. His job demands up to four restaurant visits a week so, as he puts it, he tries not to eat too much between meals. Breakfast is likely to be toast or cereal and coffee rather than too many venison sausages and he has no regular domestic routine other than that imposed by the big black cat called Benson who shares his flat in Edinburgh. But for the purpose of this interview he has designed a picnic which would be provided by one of the best hotels using the best Scottish ingredients to be eaten in the Scottish countryside.

He likes a picnic almost as much as he likes Scotland; there are three kinds of picnic, the typical Scottish weather picnic where you hide behind a boulder to get out of the wind, the 'I'm-not-going-out-in-that' picnic where you eat it in front of the fire at home and the miraculous once-in-a-while picnic when the weather is perfect.

Assuming a miraculous day he would pack a hamper with prawns - not those 'horrible little frozen prawns in sickly pink sauce' - but fresh west coast shell fish which he has been told you should devour entirely, if you can bring yourself to dip your little finger in to bring out the best part, the brains. There would be game pie, and smoked salmon - smoked pigeon breast is tempting too but would overdo the game; Scottish goats' cheese, plenty of real home-made bread, bottles of wine ('that is where I would draw the line at Scottish produce'). For pudding there might be soft fruit or butterscotch ice-cream and strawberries soaked in Drambuie and orange juice, 'just an idea', and maybe a fruit pie too.

There would be plenty of friends. 'Conversation makes a meal' says the man whose heart sinks when the head waiter approaches him and asks 'Table for one, Sir?' 'You are taken to a table which is invariably placed next to the kitchen or plonked right in the middle of the room.'

There would be no sorbet, one of his aversions ('it is supposed to refresh the palate but all it does is ruin the taste of the wine'), no biscuits and no packet soup. Best of all there would be no particular rules or ceremonies - Neil especially enjoys picnics because they are informal.

Kirsty Burrell chooses family food which can be prepared quickly and easily. She finds that supermarket trips are seldom worth the effort and prefers to shop locally for fish, meat, fuits and vegetables. Colourful, imaginative presentation of food for family and friends is a hallmark of her style which can have the effect of turning a simple meal into a celebration

Kirsty Burrell discovered that she loved cooking when she had nothing else to do on Saturdays but spend the day shopping and preparing for a long, leisurely lunch with friends on Sunday.

That was when she was a single primary school teacher living in Woking, 'where there was really nothing much else you could do at weekends'. Now she has two children, a part-time job, and active outdoor Sundays which do not leave much time for lunch. But she still loves cooking and believes meals should be shared, so she has developed a seemingly effortless style of cooking for her family and friends based on a simple idea: if you buy the best quality meat and fish, 'and that is easy to find in Scotland', you don't have to do anything very fancy to come up with a good meal.

She has a few other tricks up her sleeve. The art history graduate who ran a junk shop in Edinburgh has an eye for detail which can pick out exactly the right bowl to set off the colours of the salad without laboriously arranging the lettuce and raddiccio. A plentiful supply of interesting crockery is one of her secrets; and colour is another vital ingredient in Kirsty's cooking, which you might expect from someone who works in a deep blue kitchen with double doors opening to a bright yellow dining room full of her children's paintings.

So blackberries folded into Greek yogurt not only taste good, they make a beautiful swirl of colour in a yellow bowl and take very little time to prepare. Smoked venison is a wonderfully purple quick supper starter. And there is plenty of black pudding for cooked breakfast on Sunday.

'My food is very simple,' says Kirsty. 'Lots of people, like me, are very busy so I choose things which can be prepared quickly and easily.' She has had her day of creating choux pastry swans and poaching pears in a syrup of apricots and enjoyed doing it. But although her children are at school she likes to keep afternoons for them as well as undertaking a part-time freelance job decorating her architect husband's showhouses, 'down to the last teaspoon', so food cannot dominate the day. Evening meals for the family are made between 4.00 and 6.00 pm and on weekdays it's likely to be pasta or soup. 'We make a point of having a really nice meal on Saturday evenings either with the family or friends.' On Sundays a big cooked breakfast leaves the rest of the day free but in the evening they may return from their weekend cottage to Edinburgh with a gathering of hungry friends, so a wild duck is crisped off in the oven, blackcurrants grabbed out of the freezer (perhaps in mistake for some other fruit) make a pudding with yoghurt and amaretti biscuits, 'as nice as anything I might have spent hours planning'.

The influence of Elizabeth David and European holidays shows in an approach which combines simplicity with celebration; 'celebrations are important'. Kirsty likes meals where adults and children sit down together. She has developed a family tradition of a Christmas party for a hundred guests. For this occasion she enjoys the hours of preparation with a friend, providing a baked ham with spiced plums, bowls of colourful salads and a huge dish of baked potatoes with only a brief spell of panic before guests arrive. 'Will there be enough to eat, will it all be ready in time?'

She makes it sound easy and natural but cooking was not part of her own childhood in Ayrshire. 'My mother did not enjoy cooking. Food was ordered over the phone and it was always roast beef on Sunday, cold on Monday.' Kirsty taught herself to cook by reading Elizabeth David 'working my way through from one end of her books to the other'. She likes the down to earth approach, the slightly acid-edge to the writing, 'she is not at all a sweet little old lady'. The basic principle echoes the best modern Scottish cooking: good food is simple, fresh and seasonal.

There is very little tinned food in Kirsty's store cupboard apart from tinned tomatoes, and tinned kidney beans which can bulk up a stew when unexpected guests arrive. She makes rowan jelly and herb vinegars in season. The freezer carries vegetables from the weekend cottage, wax cartons of herbs, because she believes the flavour survives freezing better than drying, and the odd packet of frozen peas. But on the whole she prefers to buy food as she needs it from local shops - whether it is sea trout or home-cured bacon - avoiding supermarkets if at all possible. 'I always regret going to the supermarket, it isn't cheaper or easier at all in the end, and there is nothing like going to a fishmongers for fresh fish. In Scotland we have the best choice of fresh fish - if you go early in the morning you see boxes of beautiful fish arriving and it is all sold that day.'

Fashions for lighter food have influenced most people; smaller portions of meat and yogurt, rather than cream, for many puddings. 'But I still very much like the kind of European peasant food which has gone out of favour, with spicy sausages and chick peas - wonderful warm nourishing food.' In summer, dinner is likely to end with a homemade fruit ice-cream, but in winter Kirsty makes something rich and gooey with chocolate.

When her children were very young, the evening meal had to be prepared early, 'it was too depressing trying to cook in the afternoon,' but now that Duncan and Clarinda are older they often cook with her ('I have always thought it was safer if they learned how to work with sharp knives') and each can present a meal. Duncan does a very good stuffed tomato. 'He has learned there is a theatrical side to cooking and has found that bringing in the dish with the food nicely presented gets congratulations from everyone and that is very nice.'

Ecologist Tess Darwin is researching the traditional uses of Scotland's wild plants in food, medicine and folklore. She collects flowers, herbs and berries from the countryside near her Balerno home and tries out recipes in the family kitchen

Tess Darwin would like to live in a country cottage with roses round the front door and a garden full of flowers and vegetables but since that is an elusive dream the brick town house in a new estate has unexpected advantages for an ecologist who explores the wide open spaces for wild food.

There is only a tiny strip of garden round the house but the estate is on the edge of open countryside stretching to the Pentland Hills, good hunting ground for the educated eye to find delicacies the average wellington boot would tread on. Seasons are celebrated in the changing flavours brought back from expeditions into the wild beyond the suburban sprawl of Balerno, outside Edinburgh. Young nettles in spring for soup, summer clovers to enhance salad, sweet cicely to flavour fruit drinks, wild raspberries and strawberries to pick and eat, best of all autumn for

blackberry pies, elderberry cordials, rowan jellies, rose hip syrups, and - when you know what you are looking for - wide varieties of mushrooms to transform omelettes or eat on their own spiced with nutmeg. A weekend walk might bring back a margarine tub full of chanterelles.

Tess Darwin, an ecologist, is married to another ecologist, Ian Edwards, who works at Edinburgh's Royal Botanic Garden and they have the experience of wildlife management in Malawi behind them. There, mangoes fall off the trees and wayside stalls are loaded with fruit and vegetables which takes away some of the need to search the wilderness. Ian first introduced Tess to wild food when they were both working in the Scottish Highlands. Now with her children, Hazel and Robin, out to school and nursery in the mornings she is taking the opportunity of home-based work to research the traditional uses of wild plants in Scotland in food, medicine and folklore. That means hours in the library, or trying to find old people with memories of traditions and superstitions almost forgotten, and experiments with food back home in the kitchen as she tries out old recipes and wild plants even she had not thought of before. 'Eight different kinds of seaweed used to be eaten in the Hebrides, now the most common ones in use are dulse and carrageen.'

Wild food fits a vegetarian diet and a way of life devoted to preserving the countryside. Tess became a vegetarian when she was a teenager not just because of a moral objection to killing animals, but also because of the wasteful use of resources and the unequal division of the spoils of the planet between the rich and poor countries.

She is, she says, a natural vegetarian, 'giving up meat was no hardship to me', and if she did not have growing children to cater for would like to be a vegan, cutting out eggs and dairy food. But cheese and eggs are a good source of protein for children so they form half of the basic family diet with the other half coming from nuts, beans and pulses.

Like other cooks in this book she taught herself to cook. 'My mother was careful to give us good, nourishing food but she did not really enjoy cooking.' Tess does enjoy providing tasty and interesting food for her family but because meals fit into a full day (both parents run evening classes and take part in local community life) she allows roughly an hour for cooking and the family sits down to the evening meal around 5.30 pm. They eat pasta (the children enjoy it with a nut, tomato and mushroom sauce), vegetable casseroles, rice and millet bakes and lots of salads. In winter especially, they grow bean sprouts and make bowls full of 'anything you can grate' often with apples and bananas added and yoghurt dressing.

Herbs are an essential part of whole food. Tess likes to add chives, mint or marjoram to salads, and serves stuffed eggs on a bed of lovage leaves to absorb flavour. Puddings are often fruit salads (mango purée makes a naturally sweet alternative to syrup), pies in autumn and winter, or fruit stirred into crowdie and topped with toasted oatmeal.

Weekends are for entertaining. Tess likes to make meals to share with friends on Saturday nights and enjoys it best when she can provide a buffet for people to help themselves once the children are in bed. 'If I make a sit-down dinner which I have to serve I find I am thinking about it all the time whereas if I can just set it out and leave it I can sit down and relax with everyone else and enjoy the company.' For Christmas or special occasions they might have a *pâté en croute* (walnuts and mushrooms flavoured with wine in pastry) with baked chestnuts and vegetables in a sauce, 'and I have a passion for roast potatoes'.

Tess makes cakes rich in fruit - apples, plums as well as dried fruit - and has found a recipe which substitutes tinned pineapple for sugar. Ian bakes most of the bread. They shop at whole food wholesalers and organic grocery shops in Edinburgh but supermarkets now also supply some of the widest ranges of exotic fruit and vegetables. Tess keeps a store of dried foods and cereals, a liquidiser to make light work of chopping nuts but does not yet have a freezer. When they get the allotment they hope to have, she says it will make sense to freeze some of what they grow.

But one of the values of collecting wild food is that it keeps you in touch with the changing seasons. 'It makes you part of the countryside, not just an observer and it also makes you realise how strong natural flavours are compared with the blandness of mass-produced fruit and vegetables. To me the most interesting thing about the traditional recipes using wild things is that the wild ingredient is the flavouring of the meal, it does not want to be disguised at all.'

Entertaining for both business and pleasure has become a way of life for Sandra Macpherson of Glentruim who acts both as cook and hostess to visitors at the family's baronial mansion near Newtonmore

The capercaillie is a lucky bird. *Tetrao urogallus*, the largest grouse, which may be mistaken for an airborne turkey, is just about the only species of game on the estate which has not ended up in **Sandra Macpherson of Glentruim's** kitchen to be dressed, cooked and, when occasion demands, piped into dinner by a piper in full highland regalia.

Hare, deer, duck, snipe, and the common-or-garden grouse are not spared. Rabbits make a superb curry (and there are plenty of curries bobbing round the rhododendrons across the lawns) and Sandra has been known to stand for hours in the river to catch her own salmon for supper. 'But we have never shot a capercaillie,' she says. 'They are very friendly, a little rare, and one used to strut up and down the drive.'

Visitors, especially those from Japan and America, love it all. There is no doubt that the baronial setting and rich bag of game provided by her husband's inheritance has helped to create Sandra Macpherson's growing international reputation as Scottish cook and hostess. Proud of her family's

Scottish heritage, she likes to put on a good show and guests at the nineteenth century neo-baronial house are usually treated to preprandial bagpipes by the piper and, after dinner, a clarsach recital by the hostess.

But the books, the recipes, the endless dinners, lunches and suppers at home, and growing invitations to organise exhibitions of Scottish food in foreign places, would not be possible if Sandra had not discovered an unsuspected love for cooking and a natural ability to cook imaginatively from the ingredients around her. It came as a surprise to her; when she was a child her mother had a cook so she hardly had to go into the kitchen. She moved to the Highlands as a newly married ex-nurse to be thrown into the deep end of a castle kitchen with no nearby shops to fall back on and the horror of her first culinary failure fresh in her mind. 'It was a disastrous Sunday lunch, roast lamb, new potatoes and peas - the lamb was the wrong cut, the peas were burnt and the potatoes would have been alright but I picked rose leaves instead of mint and they turned pink.'

She read her way through the cookery books she found in the house, Mrs Beeton and her like. She taught herself the basics and when her husband said, 'not roast pheasant again', she knew it was time to try something different. She began to experiment. She is sure that certain flavours just go naturally together and is irritated by recipe books which attribute names like *coq au vin* to dishes which very likely emerged of their own accord in Scottish kitchens too. Recently she devised a combination of chicken and oysters feeling that the flavours were right and was delighted to find it written down in an old Scottish cookery book when she was researching at the library. Smoking and salting are traditional aspects of Scottish food too so she is determined not to be overawed by a Scandinavian name like gravadlax and insists that marinating trout in dill achieves results as good as with salmon.

Like other mothers she had to combine cooking and creating in the kitchen with bringing up children. Her son and daughter are now away at school but she has developed short cuts which she says can transform simple food with wonderful effect. The local shops are better stocked now than when she first moved north, but a shopping expedition to find a simple ingredient could mean a round trip of 15 or 20 miles; if the fish van arrives when she is out she chases after it around the glens. The deep freeze and the labour-saving food processor are essential. 'Because I always seem to be so busy I have found very easy ways of making simple food look superb.' Smoked salmon in aspic for starters, or fish mousse with decoration piped on at the last moment, brioche in the shape of a salmon, or a central display of motor bikes cut from bread to feed the visitors from Yamaha.

Less adventurous souls might quail at such tasks; Sandra insists that it is easy (aspic comes in packets) but she perhaps possesses some natural advantages. Unlike most people she does not test her food by tasting as she goes along but prefers to rely on her sense of smell: 'you can smell sweet and sour, whether there is too much pepper and so on'. The food happens so spontaneously she finds it hard when it comes to writing recipes (she broke off from her word processor for this interview): 'really, I need someone following me round the kitchen with a notebook to write it down at the time'. She loves the invention and the preparation and likes to be left alone in the kitchen to make as much mess as is necessary ('but it is wonderful to have someone else to clear it away').

Entertaining is part of the Macpherson way of life both for business and pleasure. For big official functions Sandra prefers buffets for more than thirty - the time and effort goes into thinking up the meal and the last minute touches so she would rather do it for a large number. The basics may be prepared and stored in the deep freeze days in advance but for the last minute touches on the day of a lunch Sandra gets up at 5.00 am. What she likes best of all, 'when I am able to be really selfish', is to cook something special for just two other close friends and dish it up in the kitchen by candlelight.

Sometimes she has smelled too much food all day to be able to eat anything more than a boiled egg. But when she is tired and hungry, when some of us might reach for baked beans, she will rustle up a simple quick treat of mussels and bacon with salad. Is it at all significant that the mating call of the capercaillie is described in one bird book as ending with a sound 'like drawing a cork and pouring liquid out of a narrow-necked bottle'? You couldn't shoot that.

FOCUS ON CHEESE

Joanna Blythman

The late 1980s is an exciting time for Scottish cheesemaking. All over the country one can witness the arrival of a new wave of artisan cheeses, made on a small scale by committed producers who know and love their art. And the recognition that Scotland is slowly but surely rediscovering its cheesemaking potential is doubly special when one remembers not so distant days when Scottish traditional cheese was moribund, and mass-produced creamery cheddar dominated.

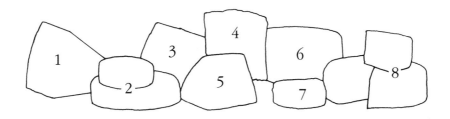

1 Isle of Mull cheddar; 2 Bonchester, Hawick; 3 Dunsyre Blue, Lanarkshire; 4 Errington Special, Lanarkshire; 5 Lanark Blue; 6 Stitchill, Kelso; 7 Nairn ewe's cheese; 8 Robrock, Huntly

Small producers are still faced with the enduring problem of commercial viability. Unlike the farmer who sells milk direct to the Milk Marketing Board for a guaranteed price, the farmhouse cheesemaker must first make an investment in equipment, cope with cash flow problems while stocks mature, and take responsibility for all stages of the marketing process. There is no special help or subsidy for any of this, and one wonders at the staying power of people who take on the task.

Another cause for excitement is the constantly improving quality of the cheeses on offer. All innovative cheesemaking is experimental and in the first instance, although the will to make fine cheese was apparent, results were often disappointing. Now it seems that mistakes have been analysed and understood, and the products have improved by leaps and bounds. So much so, that we can now justifiably claim that Scotland has a dynamic repertoire of cheeses, fit to rub shoulders with better established cheese-producing countries.

COW'S CHEESE

Many of Scotland's traditional farmhouse cheeses were made from cow's milk, and it still holds an important place as the raw material for our new cheeses. Bonchester, made near Hawick was one of the forerunners. It resembles a small Brie or Coulommiers when tasted at a perfect stage of ripeness. Stichill comes from Kelso and is made from the milk of Jersey cows. It seems to combine to great advantage the crumbly rich characteristics of authentic Wensleydale with the refreshing tartness of farmhouse Cheshire or Lancashire. Dunsyre Blue is a rich, buttery, blue cheese made from the milk of Ayrshire cows. A fortuitous experimental offshoot of Dunsyre is Errington's Special. It is less firm and more volatile than Dunsyre, and makes a meltingly seductive Scottish answer to *Gorgonzola Dolce*. Both Dunsyre and Errington's have cooking as well as cheeseboard potential because of their ability to melt successfully.

Two cheeses stand out in the tradition of farmhouse cheddar. Isle of Mull, made outside Tobermory, is a classic nippy cheese, and Gowrie, named after the Carse of Gowrie from which it hails, packs the same hearty punch. Like all good cheddars, demand outstrips supply and so the cheese is often sold before it reaches optimum maturity. Both of these cheeses are still worthwhile, even in a relatively immature state. Shapinsay differs slightly from the cheddar formula. It is not so much one cheese as a collective name for Orkney farmhouse cheese, made from cow's milk pooled from the small surrounding islands. It has a softer consistency than Cheddar, with a mild but appetising flavour.

GOAT'S CHEESE

Cheeses made from goat's milk are a very recent addition to the scene. They have no traditional pedigree, but this has not prevented them from becoming the fastest growing sector of Scottish farmhouse cheese production. Lovers of mild, creamy goat's cheese will enjoy Robrock made near Huntly. It comes in different forms, wine-dipped, vine-wrapped and blue veined, but the common feature is a light, almost lemony freshness. Benachie, from the same stable as Robrock, has strong similarities to *Sainte Maure*, the classic French goat log, and is no less successful. Ben Wyvis, made just north of Inverness, is a more crumbly and overtly 'goaty' cheese. It is even more in the style of French *Chevres Pyramides*. It comes either plain or with the addition of fresh chives. Ben Wyvis is perfect for crumbling over salads as well as serving on a cheeseboard. Two firmer goat's cheeses are worth noting. Maddoch is an ash-dusted, slightly drier cheese with a pronounced goaty flavour which is made in Perthshire. Isle of Sanday, made in Orkney, has an attractive blue-grey rind enclosing a rich, complex 'goat' flavour which becomes even more attractive as it matures.

SHEEP'S CHEESE

This is perhaps the most testing and under-developed section for new Scottish cheese. In its youth, ewe's milk can produce mild, slightly sweet cheeses which are delicious when fresh, but which are prone to dry out rapidly with no good effect. Cheeses of the standing of *Parmigiano Reggiano*, where young ewe's milk cheese has been aged and matured with skill, remain an art, and Scotland has not yet thrown up a likely candidate. But our best single success story to date is a ewe's milk cheese. Lanark Blue, from Lanarkshire, is made in the style of that other ewe's cheese classic, *Roquefort*. It is a cheese which varies with the season and is arguably best in the summer months when it reaches a pinnacle of unctuous 'blueness'. Another favourite of some years' standing and repute was Barac, made at Annan. It has the ewe's milk special sweetness with a subtle, nutty flavour. Craigrossie, from Perthshire, is surprisingly full-bodied with developed acidity and 'bite'.

So these are some of the real Scottish cheeses on offer. Seek them out and taste them if you can, but bear in mind two points. First, that cheeses of this kind are made almost exclusively from unpasteurised milk. It is this raw milk which lends the cheeses their particular character and flavour. Second, that real cheese is seasonal and will vary according to the richness of the pasture on which the animals are grazing. So do not expect a standardised, consistent result. Be prepared for your newly discovered favourite to become unavailable for a period when milk stocks are low. Above all, enjoy like me, those special occasions when you savour a Scottish artisan cheese in peak condition, with all its intriguing nuances. This kind of experience is all the more precious in a world where so much of our food has become mass-produced and characterless.

SPRING CHEFS

BETTY ALLEN

cream of courgette & rosemary soup

mousseline of scallops

with champagne & chive sauce

potatoes baked in cream with garlic

onion marmalade to serve with roast lamb

orange & grand marnier terrine

rich warm chocolate gateau

CHARLES PRICE

scottish spring lamb with savoy cabbage

pear & whisky syllabub with soft wild fruits

ALISON PARSONS

tweed kettle

or baked fillet of salmon with mushrooms

goat's cheese in filo pastry

with basil & pinenuts

SPRING TABLE

quail egg salad

supper eggs

roast rack of spring lamb

with herb or mint apple jelly

spring lemon cake

lemon curd

HONEY IN THE GROUND

nettle broth

silverweed bannocks

fat hen flan

birch sap wine

TRADITIONAL TABLE

clear hare soup

marinated trout

chicken in oyster sauce

rhubarb meringue tart

Quail egg salad
on a primrose bank

Spring in Scotland is a personal thing. It is there when you decide that it has arrived. For some people it might come as early as the first snowdrop in the garden, or the first taste of spring lamb, or a glimpse of blossom from a train window, or a walk through fields studded with wild hyacinths and primroses beside Port Appin.

Take the road there from Ballachulish, turn the last corner before the village for a view down over Stalker Castle, the island of Shuna on one side, Lismore on the other, to find the hillsides massed with ranks of purple rhododendrons. Then follow the road down to Airds Hotel and **Betty Allen**.

Betty Allen is one of our best self-taught cooks. She was brought up in Blackridge, West Lothian. 'My mother was a good cook and we always had a good vegetable garden behind the house. But I only started cooking seriously after I married Eric and we opened our first hotel in Largs.' Now she is one of only two Scots to have been made Chef Laureate for services to British cooking.

Airds Hotel stands on the shores of Loch Linnhe, so seafood is an important part of Betty Allen's repertoire, and Loch Linnhe prawns in particular, which she says taste better in the colder

weather. She buys the rest of her fish mostly from Mr Binnie in Oban who gets them from the small inshore boats that fish our west coast waters.

Turbot is particularly good. She poaches it, then serves it with a tarragon sauce or with a sauce made from wholegrain mustard from Arran. She also loves to prepare herring, our most underrated fish, soused or rolled in oatmeal. The first salmon of the year become available in April from Sandy McGlaughlin at Cuill Bay.

But although the first of the new season's vegetables are beginning to come up in the Allen's polythene tunnels beside the house, it is still mainly winter produce on the menu this far north: parsnips, carrots and winter cabbage for much of early spring.

Charles Price knows all about good spring shellfish from northern waters. He worked for a while at Kyle of Lochalsh with chef Paul Rogerson. 'There was a local man called Ally the Clam who used to supply the hotel with scallops the size of two hands together.' Charles would dip the scallops in unsalted butter, roll them in fresh breadcrumbs and herbs, then grill them with hazelnut or wild garlic butter. He also found good lobster and crayfish in the spring.

After a childhood in Drumchapel in Glasgow, Charles Price trained first at the Fountain Restaurant and then Gleneagles. Now he can be found in Gleddoch House, a country house hotel at Langbank overlooking the Clyde, between Clydebank and Port Glasgow. In springtime the fields round Gleddoch House are awash with daffodils and crocuses. Thyme, fennel, marjoram and other herbs are beginning to come through in his garden, and the rosemary is in flower.

Much of his vegetable produce comes from Kippens in Glasgow, who supply the first of the season's potatoes, like Ayrshire pinks, as well as savoy cabbages which Charles considers very good if cooked properly. He usually takes the leaves off, takes out the centre stalk, cooks the whole leaves

Facing: seafood is an important part of chef laureate Betty Allen's repertoire; Charles Price (above left) is constantly seeking new ways of preparation which do not mask the character of the food he prepares in season; Alison Parsons favours hogget over spring lamb

until tender, refreshes them in cold water, dries them and then stuffs them with a forcemeat for braising in a gravy, or wraps them round a vegetarian parcel to serve with nutmeg sauce.

But it is Scotch lamb that Charles Price associates with spring. His butcher, Drew Mackenzie of Robert Alexander in Port Glasgow, supplies him with the best of lamb from the Ayrshire hills. These are Suffolk sheep - 'a real butcher's sheep with a good covering of fat,' says Drew. Charles' philosophy is to interfere as little as possible with good food - such as the gigot of the lamb or the tender eye of the loin - but he is always looking for new ways of presentation which do not mask the character of the food.

Alison Parsons' spring is even later than most. Polmaily House Hotel, which she runs with her husband Nick, sits in a frost trap in Glen Urquhart near Drumnadrochit, and it takes a while for the warmer weather to reach her door.

In the early months she prepares hogget, (one year old sheep), more than spring lamb. It is not mutton but it has a stronger taste then the new season's lamb and she likes the flavour. She cooks

only the best end and serves it whole with garlic puree or with last year's gooseberry jelly.

It seems to be the animals and birds Alison keeps at Polmaily that decide when spring has come, and particularly the ducks, which start to lay eggs for breakfast between April and June. If there is such a thing as an ideal Scottish breakfast to keep the cold weather at bay, then those free range duck eggs deserve a place on the menu.

Dr Johnson once reflected that an epicure seeking sensual gratification need look no further than the Scottish breakfast. With his duck eggs he might have best Glentarkie bacon, white pudding from Duncan Fraser of Inverness and the excellent black pudding made in Stornoway on the island of Lewis. With the addition of some sausages, beef or venison, from Michael Sheridan in Ballater and some of Alison's homemade potato scones he would have something close to Highland Nirvana.

Of course, all this would follow a lightly smoked haddock with warm oatcakes from Forbes Bakery at Muir of Ord spread with raspberry preserve or heather honey from Struan Apiaries at Conon Bridge.

SPRING TABLE

Kirsty Burrell

A Japanese friend who stayed with me at one time told me that in Japan people have blossom-watching parties in spring. My beautiful old pear tree had just come into flower, so we decided to have one too. I made a cake which has since become a family favourite for spring celebrations - a lemon-flavoured pound cake, decorated with a flowery 'sprig' of mimosa and angelica, drizzled over with a syrup of caster sugar and lemon juice. The top hardens to become crunchy and the lemo. flavour soaks into the cake, giving a sharp, fresh, not too sweet flavour which appeals even to people who do not normally like cakes.

Jane Grigson, in her beautiful *Fruit Book*, says that in her childhood they used to be given homemade lemonade as a late winter drink to 'cleanse the blood' and revive them with its freshness after stodgy winter food. Nowadays we would drink this as a summer refresher, with ice and a sprig of mint or borage, but you can make it in early spring when lemons are cheap and plentiful, because it stores well in waxed cartons in the freezer, as does lemon curd.

Springtime is egg time: the children hunting in the garden for chocolate eggs before breakfast on Easter Sunday (the sharp-eyed observer might earlier have spotted the Easter bunny lolloping round the garden in dressing-gown and welly boots, looking for likely hiding places in the bare vegetable plot!); then sitting round the kitchen table colouring hard boiled eggs with wax crayons. One year we had beautiful pale blue duck eggs, and last year we had goose eggs - more scope for artistic endeavour. Many children in Scotland still roll decorated eggs - ancient symbols of fertility - down grassy slopes on Easter Sunday morning; surely a link with a pre-Christian past, though some theologians see the practice as 'symbolising the rolling away of the stone from the mouth of the tomb at Gethsemane'.

This year Lisbeth McGaffin of The Mill Shop in Aberfeldy, assembled a diverse and beautiful

Perthshire eggs in baskets (clockwise from bottom left): goose and turkey; blackhack, duck and leghorn; Orkney, aritkner and guinea fowl and quail eggs on a mossy stone. Next page: lemon flavoured pound cake decorated with a flowery sprig of mimosa and angelica

29

collection of edible eggs, all gathered in Glen Lyon one Sunday. When she called at a house to collect the turkey eggs none were available, but as she was leaving, the children came rushing in to say that one of the turkeys had obliged! It would be a shame to deprive any of these eggs of their shells before serving them, but it would be worth inventing little lunch dishes for them - nests of frizzy endive and radicchio with a dressing of walnut oil and herb vinegar - and people could shell their own - hard boiled, but only just. Quails' eggs, once a rare luxury, but now widely available, are too fiddly to prepare in large numbers, but make ideal snacks for special picnics. A 'bacon and egg' salad, with salad vegetables of different colours and textures, hard boiled quails' eggs and crispy little strips of fried smoked streaky bacon thrown on at the last minute would make a delightful starter for an Easter meal. Tiny bantams' eggs make treats for children, fried - like a daisy on a plate.

In the past every major Scottish house and farm had its 'doocot' (many now remain as decorative ruins) which played a crucial role in assuring a supply of fresh eggs and the occasional bird through the winter. The early spring months were the period when food for humans and livestock alike was at its most meagre, and the austerity of Lent made a virtue of necessity. In these days of comparative plenty, people are eating lighter meals from choice rather than necessity. I must admit that I am daunted, reading old Scottish recipe books, by the plethora of recipes for such dishes as potted hough and sheep's heid. I find, on the whole, that, rather than spend hours transforming some cheap cut of meat into a wholesome dish, I regard meat as a luxury and buy good cuts for weekend meals or entertaining friends. On weekday evenings we tend to have soup with yogurt and grated cheese or croutons, pasta or something eggy. One family favourite is eggs baked with cream, with plenty of fresh tarragon or chervil, served with a green salad, and a bran loaf is another. The eggs must be free range - they taste better and you won't have those poor battery creatures on your conscience!

Even if the weather has not warmed up by the beginning of April, I have mentally moved into spring. I want to put behind me the hearty Scotch broths and legs of lamb with haricot beans that see us through the winter, and look for a fresher, lighter taste. Spring lamb is an expensive luxury, and needs a light touch. I ask my butcher to cut a rack of lamb with the shin bone removed. This makes a neat, elegant little joint - the French *carre d'agneau* which needs only minimum cooking and is easy to carve. I loath lurid green vinegary mint sauce, and would serve apple mint jelly with this. Later when the first tiny spring vegetables appear, I would make a casserole, like the French *navarin d'agneau*, with tender lamb simmered in broth, the vegetables added to the pot at carefully graduated intervals so that they are all become tender at the same time.

When we spend time at our country cottage I give priority to going for long healthy walks with my family and do not spend hours cooped up in the kitchen making healthy stews for them. When we return, tired and hungry, I have to get my walking boots off and produce a meal in the time it takes my husband to light the fire and the paraffin lamp. My son's favourite is lamb chops (he's a carnivore, despite his tender feelings towards the 'wee lammies') lightly grilled, with butter mashed up with lemon juice and plenty of chopped mint and parsley, accompanied by a steamed medley of whatever vegetables the children can find in the vegetable plot - one courgette, a handful of mange-tout peas, some broad beans (best eaten with pods when tiny) and a show of radish-sized potatoes.

In the past the monotony of life was broken by frequent holy days and feast days - something to look forward to and prepare for; a pleasant memory of richness and drama to keep you going, and I think it is a pity that so many have been lost and forgotten, particularly in Scotland where after the Reformation, such things were regarded as 'devilish'. I try to keep the ones we still have - St Valentine's Day, Shrove Tuesday, Easter - and perhaps invent a few more 'traditions'. After Easter, though, I look forward to May Day, when I officially declare summer, ready or not!

HONEY IN THE GROUND
Tess Darwin

The list of wild foods which our ancestors knew well is very long. Conservationists, justifiably, would be upset if we went around wantonly uprooting plants, but most of those mentioned here are common in Scotland and can be gathered without destroying the plant. Some great culinary adventures can be had by looking more closely at what grows in the hedgerows and wasteland around us, and learning to turn some of these 'weeds' into delicious dishes. The modern Scottish diet is generally assumed to be superior to that of our ancestors. It comes as a surprise, therefore, to discover that a variety of wild foods eaten in earlier times added interest and nourishment to a rather monotonous basic menu. Indeed, on many occasions it was only the extensive knowledge people had about edible wild plants that saved whole communities from famine when crops failed due to disease or bad weather.

The small creeping herb **silverweed**, for example, was sought for its roots, which were very popular until potatoes became widespread, and even then it was literally a life-saver when the dreaded potato blight struck. It was known in Gaelic as *an seachdamh aran* (the seventh bread) and an old song talks about 'Honey under ground, Silverweed of spring'. Boiled or roasted, the roots taste similar to parsnips; raw, they have a crunchy, slightly nutty flavour. They can also be dried and ground into flour for bread or porridge. In some places, particularly the Western Isles, it was grown as a vegetable crop, and it was said that in North Uist a man could sustain himself on a square of ground his own length given over to silverweed.

One flower we particularly associate with spring was welcomed in earlier times for more than its beauty. **Wood sorrel** forms carpets of delicate pinkish-white flowers in damp woodland areas before the trees open their leaves. The leaves of wood sorrel are like three-leaved clover, and it is thought that this was actually the plant St Patrick used to illustrate his explanation of the Trinity of God. The bright green leaves persist well into the

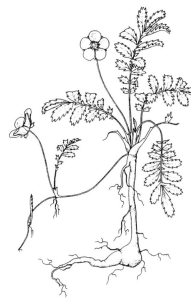

Silverweed

Wood Sorrel

summer and can be found beneath even the densest ferns. They have a sharp, fruity taste, very much like rhubarb (both contain oxalic acid). It can be imagined with what relish the leaves were eaten to stimulate taste buds jaded after a winter of stored, starchy food with little or no fresh fruit.

Many plants that we destroy as undesirable weeds were once highly esteemed for their useful qualities. **Nettles** grow rapidly in spring and besides their excellent food value, in days when people were rather preoccupied with their bodily functions (possibly a direct result of the seasonal nature of their diet) the slightly laxative and diuretic properties of nettles were greatly appreciated. The tender young shoots, gathered (wearing gloves!) when 8-10 inches (20-25 cm) high, make tasty broth which is filling if a little oatmeal is added in the traditional manner. They need to be boiled for about 20 minutes (which renders the acrid juice in the stinging hairs harmless), then sieved or liquidised because nettles are very fibrous. Indeed, nettle fibres were used until the eighteenth century for weaving household linen, as testified by the poet Thomas Campbell: 'In Scotland, I have eaten nettles, I have slept in nettle sheets, and I have dined off a nettle tablecloth'.

Another weed which was widely eaten in Scotland until spinach arrived was **fat hen**. The fatty seeds from which its name may derive are known to have been eaten in the Bronze Age. In Scots it was commonly known as smear docken (i.e. fat or grease dock) or midden mylies, from its habit of growing wherever people threw household or farmyard rubbish and manure. This does not seem to have put anyone off eating it, however, and in Gaelic it was called more graciously *pràiseach fiadhain* (wild potage). The succulent leaves make delicious soup or it can be boiled, mashed and served with butter as a nutritious green vegetable. There is no need to wade through manure to find fat hen as it grows throughout Scotland on waste and arable land.

In the same way as certain foods, like oatmeal and salmon, are characteristically Scottish, we also have some wild plants that thrive here but are rare

Fat Hen

elsewhere. **Scots lovage**, also known as sea parsley or shemis, is one example. It is similar to celery, and used to be popular in salads, as well as boiled as greens. It grows near the sea in certain parts of Scotland.

Hedgerows in southern Scotland and northern England often abound in early spring with the creamy white flowers of **sweet cicely**, but this plant is rare elsewhere. It has a delightful aroma of aniseed and a few leaves add flavour to green salad, although it should be used sparingly, since it is quite strong. People also used to eat the unripe seeds and boiled roots served with oil and vinegar. Sweet cicely was reputed to prevent plague, rejoice the heart and increase lust and strength - not to mention its usefulness for polishing oak furniture! Rub with the whole plant and allow to dry, then shine with a cloth - it leaves the wood smelling lovely too.

An unusual and exceedingly delicious dry white wine can be made very easily from the sap of one of Scotland's commonest trees, **birch**. The sap begins to rise at the beginning of spring, in early March, and can be collected from large old trees by boring a small one inch (2 cm) deep hole slanting upwards about 18 inches (45 cm) from the ground. A plastic tube which fits tightly into the hole is inserted and drains down into a one gallon (5 litre) demi-john. The neck of the jar must be sealed with tissue around the tube to keep bits and beasties out while allowing air to escape as the jar fills. A single tree should half-fill such a demi-john over-night, so two trees will supply sufficient sap for the recipe included for birch sap wine.

Sweet Cicely

CLEAR HARE SOUP

Both the common hare and the mountain hare are well known in Scotland, though their numbers have been sadly reduced in recent years due to over-shooting. In the evening and early morning the reddish brown common hare darts spectacularly through fields and copses, resting during the day in a 'form' between banks of vegetation. The slightly smaller mountain hare makes its form between rocks and stones in mountainous areas of north Scotland.

Bawd bree is a traditional recipe for hare soup, 'bawd' being the Scots for hare and 'bree' for soup. The hare was well hung, skinned and soaked in water overnight while the blood was set aside for making the bawd bree. Such robust preparations are unlikely to appeal to modern cooks, however, and a more acceptable, and delicious alternative is clear hare soup.

Quenelles make an outstanding garnish for this soup. Franco-Scottish in origin, these seasoned balls of fish or meat have been made in Scotland for several hundred years, but recently seem to have been forgotten in thir traditional form. It is interesting, though, that leading chefs and cooks in Scotland now frequently include dishes described as quenelles. Here the term refers to the spoon-shape of the food, be it sweet or savoury (see Mark Salter's Autumn recipe for ice-cream quenelles). The garnish for the soup is indeed dropped from a spoon, rather like small doughballs.

MARINATED TROUT

In the Scottish rivers, the brown trout, sea trout and salmon quietly and secretly dart from pool to pool, stopping from time to time under rock or stone. Eye holes can still be seen in the rocks at the edge of some rivers, where nets were tied to catch the fish that were to be salted and savoured in the long winters. A true fisherman would wait patiently with his rod, calmly anticipating his strike while the skilled, but hasty, poacher might simply grab the fish

from the river. Hungry, and with no implements to hand, he might make a fire out in the open, gut the trout, wrap it in wet paper and cook it in the cinders. The trout was ready when the paper was burned through - a primitive version of the modern barbecue.

Few things taste quite so delicious as freshly caught trout lightly grilled for breakfast. But if the fish is to be preserved it is worth turning to a recipe for gravadlax, a Scandanavian method which literally means 'buried salmon' and gives an equally delicate and unusual flavour to other fish, including salmon and trout.

Trout is traditionally cooked in oatmeal, or simply grilled or fried in butter and served with a wedge of lemon. Perhaps trout farming, which has made supplies of the fish plentiful, has helped to encourage new ways of preparing it. Trout stuffed in a variety of ways - with oatmeal, shellfish or herb mixtures - increasingly appear on menus, and marinated trout is a favourite.

CHICKEN AND OYSTERS

On a cold bleak day in 1861 a coach drew up at the Highland village of Dalwhinnie. The travellers who entered the inn to ask for accommodation were recognised by a maid who whispered to the innkeeper that they included none other than Queen Victoria, Prince Albert one of the Queen's wardrobe maids and Lady Churchill's maid. While the royal guests were changing out of their wet clothes, all was rush and bustle downstairs with hasty preparations for the evening meal. The table was laid, the candles lit and the royal party, hungry after their long journey, sat down to dine. The Queen was not impressed - and presumably not amused! Their supper, according to her diary, consisted of, '...only tea, and two miserable starved Highland chickens without potatoes! No pudding and no fun'. Not even the sound of the bagpipes could compensate for that unhappy evening and they retired early to bed.

Had Queen Victoria been served chicken and oysters she might have been better pleased. This is a superb dish which, according to old kitchen records, was frequently prepared. Oysters were once found in abundance all over Scotland. In *The Scots Kitchen*, F. Marian McNeill refers to evidence that 100,000 oysters were consumed every day in Edinburgh alone. Small wonder, then, that cookery books from the last century are full of recipes using oysters - in stews, pies, soups and sauces.

Now that oysters are being cultivated once more, we can look forward to exploring their potential by reviving old recipes and trying out new methods like those included in this book. Chicken with oysters is a favourite with my family. Although traditionally a lunch dish, it is perhaps even better suited to being the main course for a dinner party.

RHUBARB MERINGUE TART

The clean sharp taste of rhubarb makes an excellent sweet to compliment a dinner party meal. Rhubarb is usually readily available. It will flourish with little or no cultivation and has always been very popular in Scotland. Although there was plenty of protein in the eighteenth century there was a great lack of fruit and vegetables which caused a vitamin C deficiency. Early medical books often recommended treatment with a dose of rhubarb both as a purge and to replace vitamin C.

Abundant as it was, cooks used every stick for puddings, jams and chutneys. The first crop in spring, sweeter and more tender, is best for the delicate sweets and puddings, leaving later crops for dumplings, jams and chutneys. Syllabub was frequently made with rhubarb and whipped cream and rhubarb fool with custard and cream. Raw rhubarb, chopped and sprinkled with sugar, keeps beautifully in the deep freeze, ready for making into jams and chutneys at leisure. There is no need to rush to cook it in the busy summer when the crops become adundant.

Scots kitchens produced rhubarb tarts of all kinds, some with pastry lining the dish, others with a pastry lid as well. The pastry might be simple or extremely decorative, and occasionally custard was poured into the middle of the crust. Rhubarb tarts with meringue toppings were also popular and a variation of this - a rhubarb tart encased with meringue makes a delicious cold or hot pudding.

FOCUS ON FISH

Joanna Blythman

When I was a child in Glasgow in the late 1950s and 1960s, we ate fish religiously once a week. Religiously in two senses, because Protestants ate it on Wednesdays and Catholics ate it on Fridays.

It was always haddock, shallow-fried in ersatz orange breadcrumbs served with chips. Otherwise our glimpses of the potential feast of fish were *sole bonne femme*, reserved for dinner parties, or a rare crab or two, transported back from seaside holidays.

This monotonous approach, which was very widespread, did nothing to endear fish to me. It was just part of unexciting weekday routine. The fact that our lochs and shores were teeming with delicious varieties of fish and shellfish, simply washed over me. Langoustines, oysters, razor clams, brill or scallops only impinged via the pages of Elizabeth David, not as part of any day to day reality. The local fish shop offered little in the way of inspiration. Here the traditional Scottish favourites, fresh haddock, sole and herring, were the staples. Fish such as mackerel, monkfish and cod were seen as 'English', and by implication, not worth eating.

This highly conservative approach to fish retailing is still at the heart of Scotland's ambivalence towards fish. Commentators on the state of our fish trade have described Scottish fishmongers as interested only in selling haddock to fish and chip shops, with very limited horizons and an unwillingness to take a risk. And indeed, it does seem that the largest part of our current trade in less workaday fish and seafood bypasses established the Scottish wholesale fish markets.

But retailers are not the only problem. The buying public is too. Historically the Scots have consumed a great deal of fish, but it has never been regarded as a high status foodstuff, with the possible exception of lobster and salmon. Fish was popular when it was cheap, but short-sighted over-fishing and belated attempts at conservation have meant that the price of even basic fish has soared, particularly in relation to meat. White fish sales have dropped, sixty per cent of the population never eat fish, and the

recession in retailing can be witnessed as more and more small shops give up the battle and disappear.

Yet just as the market in staple white fish has contracted, so the sales and interest in our indigenous, less familiar fish and shellfish has grown. The fish buying public in Scotland has become more streamlined, composed of dedicated consumers, seeking out better and more ambitious ranges. We have learnt through cookery books and foreign holidays that fish can be fun and healthy to boot, and the more we learn, the more we experiment.

For the enterprising shopper, shellfish is still the most difficult of all Scottish foodstuffs to pin down. Highly perishable, it comes in as a pricey commodity. Because Scottish shellfish is such a superior product, it attracts premium prices both in the rich market of the south east of England, Europe and even further afield, so producers see little need to woo the stubborn and often stingy home market.

Ironically, you may well find it easier to experience Scottish shellfish on a holiday on the Costa del Sol than in the Western Isles.

In an attempt to eliminate waste, the shellfish which appears in our local fishmongers will more than likely be frozen, or boiled, so destroying its sweet and subtle flavours.

There is still endless scope for expanding the repertoire of fin fish and shellfish on offer in our local fishmongers. As supplies of the traditional white fish favourites diminish because of scarcity or imposed quotas, our best hope is the development of fish farming.

Scotland's lochs and shorelines provide exceptionally pure water, with enviably low levels of arsenic, lead, cadmium and mercury. This is an ideal environment for fish cultivation, as the success story of farmed salmon over the last decade shows.

Now Atlantic salmon, once an expensive luxury is easily obtainable and affordable for most people. Clean, fine-shelled mussels, grown on ropes in the Outer Hebrides and Western Isles are another notable success story. *Giga* oysters, cultivated in waters such as Loch Fyne, give us a year round supply to compensate for the lack of native oysters. Like scallops of all sizes, while you may not

rely on finding them by chance at your local shop, you should be able to order them without any difficulty.

Experiments in farming fin fish such as halibut, turbot, sea bass and sea bream are well underway, and by the late 1990s, it may well be that these currently prized and prohibitively priced commodities will also grace the Scottish fishmonger's slab.

But the less successful example of farmed rainbow trout should also alert us to the dangers of intensive fish farming. If the end product is a flabby, muddy flavoured fish, then increased availability is unwelcome. Instead slow, steady progress with farmed fish and shellfish, with scrupulous attention to any unforeseen environmental side effects, must be taken on by the fish farming industry. If short term return and instant profit becomes the goal, then fish farmers will be in the same boat as our traditional fishing industry, asking what went wrong, too late.

Facing: fishing boat, Pittenweem harbour

SUMMER CHEFS

PETER JACKSON

squat lobster raviolis

with a sea-urchin sauce

best end of lamb with mushroom sauce

courgette tarts   potato cakes

broccoli & walnut mousse

summer fruit 'soup' with banana mousse

BRUCE SANGSTER

chilled roulade of smoked salmon

& sole mousse

parcels of wild salmon & turbot

JOHN NOBLE

fresh oysters

oysters & bacon

oysters grilled with cheese

oysters with white wine

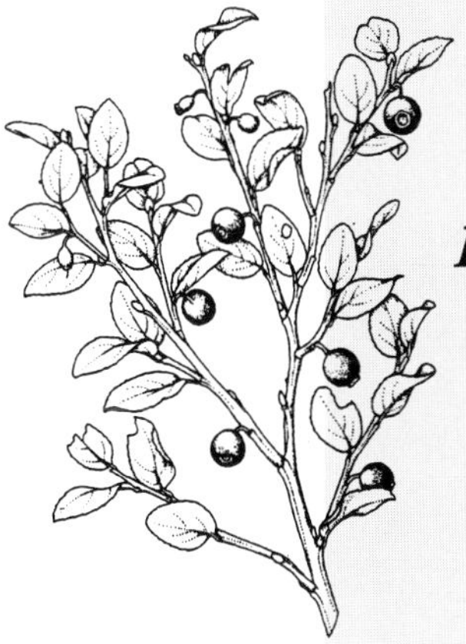

PICNICS & PARTIES

festive cassata

marquise alba

delicate green sauce

summer fruit ice creams & sorbets

white wine refresher

cullen skink   picnic beef

gooseberry sauce

kipper pâté

SAMPHIRE & SOUKIE SUMMER

watercress & potato potage

sorrel sauce

blaeberry tart

cream crowdie

TRADITIONAL MENU

partan bree

crowdie eggs

crown roast lamb & skirlie

cranachan choux

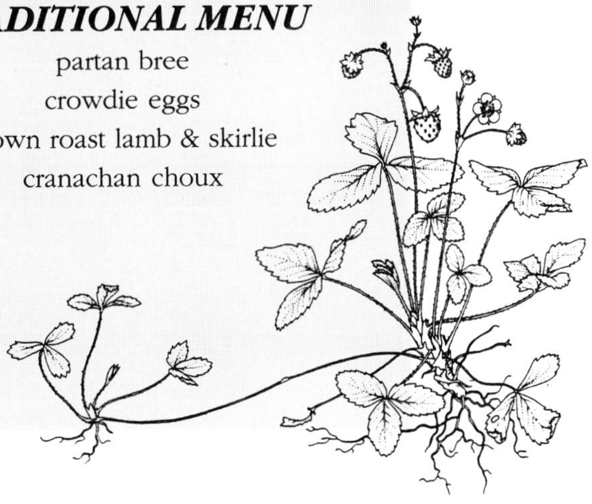

Perthshire goat's cheeses
decorated with wild flowers

SUMMER CHEFS

Neil MacLean

If we had long, hot, dry summers we would be growing vines on parched and stony ground or raking our glens with rows of olive trees - the sort of things that delight us when we travel. But would we want them here at home? The compensation for unreliable, frequently wet summers is our fine natural larder, abundant in glories like soft fruits, wild mushrooms and unrivalled Scottish beef. And when we dip a toe into the summer sea only to find it more than a little bracing, there is the consolation of the wonderful seafood which springs from its sparkling waters.

A selective memory is an asset, too. A particular heat haze above the pretty Solway village of Rockcliffe is as unforgettable as Edinburgh shimmering below Arthur's Seat on a balmy night in August. I remember sitting on sand dunes by an empty white Hebridean beach listening to the sea and wheeling curlews; and,. another time, watching the northern sun set the sky on fire over Evie and Rendall from the Orkney island of Shapinsay.

Jean Wallace makes traditional Orkney cheeses on Shapinsay. She has a small herd of cattle on Girnigoe Farm and finds the richer summer milk makes a better cheese which matures more quickly. After sitting for about ten weeks on the wooden shelves round her dairy, the cheese (pale, creamy and free from artificial colouring) is ready to be parcelled up and posted off to various destinations. Some of it goes by ferry to Kirkwall, then by road to the Stromness ferry which takes it to the Scottish mainland and, eventually, to places like **Peter Jackson's** restaurant in Glasgow.

Choosing from the cheese board is one of the highlights of eating at the Colonial Restaurant. The waiter lifts a muslin cloth and all thoughts of dessert vanish from your mind at the sight and smell of such well-tended cheeses. But by then, if you are wise, you might already have eaten his Scottish summer pudding - made from brambles, strawberries, raspberries and loganberries, or his equally luscious summer fruit soup.

Peter Jackson comes from Inverurie, near Aberdeen. He learned the value of hard work in the kitchens of Gleneagles Hotel with Chef Cottet, but feels that the place where he really learned to cook was with Paul Rogerson in Inverness. When he took his first job as a head chef he landed on his feet at Bodysgallen, the top country house hotel in Wales. To that he added the experience of visiting restaurants in London and France. But his wife became homesick and they moved back to Scotland - a move which they have not regretted. Peter opened The Colonial in 1985, and within a few months he found himself Chef Patron of the Restaurant of the Year in Glasgow.

Every night Peter Jackson's menu features a section called 'A Modern Taste of Scotland'. He finds this very easy to compile in summer. 'It's an exciting time of year. I often go up to Echo Mackenzie's farm in Duntocher to watch some of the young vegetables coming through.' He also uses some of their edible flowers in his dishes - crystallised daffodils, courgette flowers, broccoli flowers, kail flowers, nasturtiums and flowering herbs.

Peter's menus feature an abundance of fish and seafood. Six days a week he buys fresh fish from McCallums of Troon and he is particularly interested in some of the produce which fishermen tend to reject by throwing it back into the sea. Take sea urchins, for example. He uses the roe to make an unusual and delicious sauce for squat lobster raviolis. Sea urchins have a short season, between May and the end of June, he will tell you, and the roes are at their biggest when there is a full moon. He also cooks with razor clams and cockles from Mull, and buys fresh west coast lobsters to grill or cook gently in a court bouillon flavoured with red and green basil. Fishes from the warmer waters can be bought in summer and he likes John Dory, mullet and gurnet (known as groaners in the fish market because of the noise they make when they are squeezed) while turbot, halibut, brill and monkfish are also plentiful.

Peter Jackson's menus feature abundant seafood which he receives from MacCallums of Troon

The first chanterelle mushrooms appear in the Perthshire woods in July. Rosemary Thomas and Eva McDonald discovered this while walking their deerhounds. The best of the ceps start to appear in mid-August. For a short while - at least until the first frosts of Autumn - those two deerhounds become the best walked dogs in Perthshire, while the ladies pick their mushrooms. If they are really lucky and it has been a rotten Scottish summer they might find a rare mushroom called the wood hedgehog. What they don't use fresh, they dry on the kitchen table. Most of their fungi, however, find their way to Murrayshall where they are bartered by the basket for the occasional dinner for four.

The finer details of his culinary art are important to **Bruce Sangster**. Every morning a fresh batch of puff pastry is prepared in his kitchen where frozen catering packs are taboo. This pastry is often then made into little cases to hold Mrs Thomas's and Mrs McDonald's mushrooms, which are then crowned with slices of smoked Perthshire pigeon, or sometimes placed on a sauce made with slivers of truffle from East Lothian.

Bruce Sangster was born in Perth and after training with British Transport Hotels and working in the south, he became head chef at Balcraig House near Scone and then at The Murrayshall Country House Hotel close by. He is a Master Chef of Great Britain and cooks with consummate skill.

The Murrayshall estate rises to a point where you can look out across the rolling Perthshire fields, beyond to the Grampian mountains and south across the silvery Tay. Below, the hotel sits surrounded by its own golf course and Bruce's herb and vegetable gardens.

In the summer the gardens are productive and indispensable. Fresh herbs are rarely available until the warmest weather arrives, when there is also an abundance of salad leaves for the healthy gourmet - oak leaves, lamb's lettuces, lollo rosso, and Webb's lettuce. Bruce will often serve these with dressings made with his own flavoured vinegars. Some of these are made from Tayside fruits which are a feature of the area in summer when there are plenty of strawberries, raspberries, tayberries, loganberries, blackcurrants and brambles as summer wears on. Plums, too, become available and these are bottled as a treat for Christmas.

Bruce Sangster is never short of game towards the end of summer and guinea fowl and duck are best at this time of year. Like Peter Jackson, he is fond of Scottish cheeses and serves an excellent goat's milk cheese dipped in wine from Goatherd in Newtonmore. He also makes a good dressing from Dunsyre Blue to serve with fillet of lamb.

Seafood, and particularly scallops, features on his menus; he considers scallops that have been dived for finer than those that have been trawled. Langoustines, or Dublin Bay Prawns from the west are also good in summer, but - best of all - the silvery Tay is teeming with salmon.

Master Chef Bruce Sangster stresses the finer details of his culinary art. In summer his gardens are productive and indispensable

PICNICS & PARTIES

Kirsty Burrell

The best summer food is quickly prepared and eaten outside, and, better still, prepared outside too. Scottish summers are short and sunny days should not be wasted. For me, summer bliss is to sit at the table outside the back door in the afternoon sunshine, shelling peas with the help of a child or two, for a meal to be eaten later at the same table.

We have two family birthdays in June and often combine their celebration with a midsummer garden party. For a family party we might have baked sea trout with asparagus, marble sized new potatoes from the garden and hollandaise sauce, followed by a very special cake - perhaps my cassata cake or the delicious chocolate marquise alba. A bigger, grander party, however, calls for a whole salmon, baked in buttered foil, served on a bed of frizzy lettuce to look like seaweed. If it does not fit longways in your roasting tin or oven, curl it round, nose to tail and serve it that way which is both convenient and decorative. A line of cucumber 'scales' and a few twists of lemon are sufficient decoration for the king of fish. There is a splendid passage in *Summer Cooking* in which Elizabeth David berates food 'tormented into irrelevant shapes . . . and garnished with strips of this and dabs of that', finishing sternly: 'You are, after all, preparing a meal, not decorating the village hall'.

To accompany a big salmon I would fill an enormous soup tureen with tiny new potatoes, dressed, while still warm, with creamy mayonnaise and scattered at the last moment with freshly chopped chives. A couple of summer salads and a big bowl of delicate green sauce with a curly handled sauce ladle invitingly dipped in it and the core of a summer feast is there.

It is not hard to cater for a party of this kind. You need a good shopping list, and, if possible, a friend to help chop and keep you company. The result will be cheaper and probably more interesting than anything a caterer would provide, and people do appreciate it. I once prepared food for the wedding

Celebration cakes for a midsummer garden party: marquise alba (left) and festive cassata

of two friends - an idyllic June party in the garden of a cottage, with damask-covered tables swagged with roses. For my own wedding, I decorated the table in pinks and greens to enhance the food, starting with pink taramasalata, made with smoked cods' roe fresh from the fishmonger, and green guacamole (squashy avocados are ideal and often sold cheaply). Dips like these are easily made in a food processor and make good ice-breaking starters for buffets, eaten with *crudités* and bread sticks. One of my favourites, though not such a pretty colour, is *olivade* made with black olives (you can buy stoned ones in tins) and cottage cheese with a splash of malt whisky. Smoked mussels and smoked venison, cut wafer thin, make simple and appetising starters.

A barbeque in the garden is an easy way of entertaining in the summer months and, if the weather is less than sizzling, the aroma of the food can make up for it. Pockets of halved pitta bread, lightly grilled and filled with mixtures of salad, rice and meat, dispense with the need for plates - something children love. For a big party I get my butcher to make up wooden skewers of cubed lamb, which I marinate in roasting tins with olive oil, lemon juice, thyme and oregano. Monkfish is also very successful prepared in this way. Most men at parties like to do a 'stint' at the barbeque, and people enjoy filling their own pittas with salads - perhaps a big, colourful rice salad and a greek salad of lettuce, tomato and cucumber, topped with slices of feta cheese and black olives. Greek *tzaziki*, made with yogurt, cucumber and mint, goes well with spicy barbeque food.

The most popular dessert for this type of party, I find, is homemade ice cream, served in cones. (Buy delicious sugar cones from your local Italian cafe.) If you assume that only children enjoy licking ice cream from a cone, you will probably run out of them! Make a whole variety of fruit ice creams and sorbets in contrasting colours - purple blackcurrant, pink strawberry, green mint (you have to cheat a little here and add a couple of drops of green food colouring). Instead of cones you could serve them, decorated with flowers, in little glass bowls

accompanied by amaretti biscuits in their pretty wrappings.

Refreshing long drinks are appropriate served in tall glasses, tinkling with ice and decorated with fruit and mint or borage leaves. Bright blue borage flowers are so beautiful that you need no excuse to grow the plant. Pimms with lemonade and cucumber and orange slices, or a wine based drink would do. We once made our own *cassis* (very labour intensive!) from a glut of blackcurrants and had *Kir Royale* as an aperitif for summer dinner parties. On a really hot day iced coffee (slightly-sweetened good coffee, poured over crushed ice in tall glasses) would round off the party in late afternoon.

I usually take a flask of hot coffee on picnics. Even on a warm afternoon in Scotland it gets chilly as the sun drops, and grown-ups welcome a coffee before packing up and setting off, tired but happy, on the homeward journey. It seems to me that there are two distinct types of picnic, each requiring to be differently provisioned. The first is the 'posh' picnic, a *dejeuner sur l'herbe*, elegant and romantic, where no one strays far from the car or boat in which they arrived. For this kind of picnic, I have an old picnic box (complete with spirit kettle, art deco teapot and green marbled bakelite crockery) which requires a strapping chauffeur to carry it any distance. The second is more rugged; a picnic out of a rucksack, where everyone sits in walking boots by the burn munching something sustaining and well-earned. Remember the contents of Rat's 'fat, wicker luncheon basket' in one of the most successful picnics in literature (described in Kenneth Grahame's *The Wind in the Willows*): 'there's cold chicken inside it . . . coldhamcoldtonguecoldbeefpickledgherkinssaladfrench rollscresssandwichespottedmeatgingerbeerlemonade sodawater'. Circles of fruit - gooseberries, strawberries or raspberries, or an apricot mousse scattered with marigold petals would be a spectacular end to this sort of picnic. The first really requires a pre-selected spot: a flat grassy place to spread the tablecloth; an expanse of water - loch or river - in which to chill the white wine. A chilled soup such as pale green watercress or a cold version of cullen

Homemade fruit ice creams and sorbets in contrasting colours, purple, blackcurrant, pink strawberry and green mint, served with sugar cones - the most popular summer dessert

skink (the delicious Scottish smoked haddock soup) would make a good starter. If you make garlic bread just before you leave and don't take it out of the foil it should keep hot. You will need some cold meat too.

For a rugged picnic I often pack a blackened frying pan and a fire lighter in the rucksack, to cook sausages (previously grilled), bacon and black pudding. Homemade Scotch eggs, Forfar bridies or venison sausage rolls are all suitably filling and easy to eat with fingers. A favourite in our family is a thick Spanish omelette (cold) full of potatoes and onions, which can be sliced like a cake. Kipper pâté with watercress makes a delicious filling for sandwiches made from the Scottish bran loaf. A Dundee cake, oranges to be quartered and sucked and some good plain chocolate finish the meal.

These things are ideal snacks for people engaged in outdoor pursuits, while the classic snack for the pocket of the Barbour jacket is the 'shooter's sandwich': a hollowed out loaf containing a thick slice of rump steak, seasoned after grilling, flattened between sheets of greaseproof paper,

then wrapped in foil. Sliced with the gralloching knife or Swiss army knife when required, it is hearty enough to sustain the stalker, or fisherman casting his line with the river swirling round his thighs, or yachtsman adjusting the spinnaker in a shower of freezing sea water.

For day sailing in Scotland, a flask of thick hot soup is essential; cock-a-leekie or green lentil, perhaps. I much prefer to go ashore and light a fire than to cook in the galley of a keeling cruiser. In bad weather and safely in harbour, however, the well-organised cook should be able to rustle up something more delicious than tinned tomato soup. Speed is of the essence; the crew is always starving and meals are always later than planned. Pasta is a great standby. Take pesto (ground basil in olive oil) in a screwtop jar; or add cream cheese and chopped walnuts, or chopped fried streaky bacon, crushed garlic and whisked eggs.

This type of food is ideal for family cooking on a camping gas stove. I take a wooden box which can be easily lifted out of the car boot, with basic ingredients - olive oil and vinegar, salt, pepper, rice and pasta in jars, tinned kidney and haricot beans. With butter, bacon and cooking salami from the cool box I have the basis of bean stews, risottos, pasta dishes - quick one-pot meals.

Cooking in the inadequately equipped kitchen of a rented holiday cottage often presents another situation which calls for improvisation. It is worth packing some essential equipment if travelling by car: a sieve, a pepper mill, a heavy based pan for pot roasting or simmering (you can't trust an unfamiliar oven) and a couple of good kitchen knives. I take knives with me even on an airborne holiday - but not in the hand luggage. They were once picked up by the metal detecting scanner at the airport and confiscated as dangerous weapons! If you are going to a cottage in the Highlands take your own olive oil, or you'll end up buying it in tiny bottles and at great expense in the local chemist. A lump of parmesan and some cooking salami is also worth taking. Most Scottish towns have an excellent butcher selling local meat and game, and one would certainly get fresh farm eggs and, with luck, if by the sea, freshly caught fish and shellfish.

Smoked mussels and smoked venison served with delicate green sauce

SAMPHIRE & SOUKIE SUMMER
Tess Darwin

Summer was the salad season in days gone by as much as it is now, but in the absence of supermarkets full of lettuce and celery, people had to be more resourceful in creating appetising dishes.

Although now rather rare in Scotland, **rock samphire** (Gaelic *saimbhir*) was once a favourite of people in the Western Isles, where it grows on sea cliffs, rocks and shingle. The bright green plant may grow as a small bush about 12 inches (30 cm) high or hang in robust tassels; the thick, ridged stems and fleshy triangular leaves have a strong, slightly sulphurous scent. In Gaelic it was known as *lus nan cnàmh*, (the digesting weed) which has a beneficial effect on the stomach, an added bonus to its pleasant aromatic flavour. It is often pickled, but the fleshy leaves are best for salad in early summer, before the broad, mustard-yellow flower heads appear. Later the plant can be tenderised by boiling (with the stalks) for 10-15 minutes; serve with melted butter.

A similar, but unrelated edible seashore plant is marsh samphire, also known as glasswort. It grows on sandy mud in salt marshes, and is smaller than rock samphire - up to 8 inches (20 cm) tall - but usually more bushy and fleshy, with segmented rather than solid, ridged stems. It should be picked in July and August and used in the same ways as rock samphire.

Wild watercress has been well known for salads and soup at least since Roman times, and has long been sought in Scotland where it can still be gathered from clean lowland streams. The leaves can be picked at any time of year, but, having found a source of watercress, care should be taken to ensure a continuous supply by cutting only the tops of shoots and not uprooting the plant. The peppery flavour of the leaves can be best appreciated in salad or soup, but they should be washed very thoroughly before being eaten raw, as should any plant taken from water where there is always the possibility of contamination.

Sorrel is a common weed in the dock family

Sorrel

with an equally long history of use in Scotland, where it was an important source of vitamin C in days when fruit was far less freely available than it is now. Its arrow-shaped leaves can easily be found growing amidst grass on sunny banks and wasteland; they have a biting, acid taste (it was known throughout Scotland as 'sourocks'), and can be picked for salad in spring or used for sauce at any time (wood sorrel also appears in spring but looks quite different from ordinary sorrel).

Summer was the time for children to play for long hours in the sun, and they found their own refreshment in the countryside. **Wild strawberry** is a small creeping plant common along hedgerows and woodland edges; it is like a miniature version of the garden kind. The tiny bright red fruits rarely occur in sufficient quantities to make collecting for a dessert worthwhile, but their sweet flavour, so often lacking in today's forced varieties, makes them a delightful discovery. **Red clover**, too, was well known to children for the quantity of nectar the flower contains, giving it the Scots name of 'soukies' and Gaelic *sugag*. The sweet flowers and slightly bitter leaves can be added to salad, and make an eye-catching garnish.

Later in summer the long **raspberry** season begins, one of nature's finest gifts yet surprisingly few people take the trouble to collect the fruits from hedgerows where they still abound in July and August. In the past they were gathered in quantities, however, and used for punch as well as dessert and jam.

Several other plants were made into drinks in earlier times. The young shoots of **heather** took the place of hops in heather ale, brewed throughout Scotland using two-thirds heather tops to one-third malt. Dried heather flowers make an unusual herb tea, much favoured by Robert Burns. They are rich in nectar and have been used since ancient times, alone or with the addition of honey, to make a powerful kind of mead. Archaeologists working on the island of Rhum in the Hebrides recently found traces of what is thought to have been a fermented drink in pottery dating from the Stone Age. Pollen analysis suggests the recipe may have

Bog Myrtle

Blaeberry

50

included flowers of heather and meadowsweet, leaves of bog myrtle and Royal fern and oats.

The aromatic leaves of **bog myrtle** (or gale) were also used to flavour beer in the Highlands, and to make a tea said to be an effective remedy for children infested with worms! The insecticidal properties of bog myrtle made it much sought-after for strewing in beds; a bunch in the linen cupboard will keep moths away. Anyone visiting the Highlands in summer is advised to wear a sprig of myrtle behind their ears to ward off the infernal midges!

Blaeberry (or whortleberry) is a characteristic little shrub of Scottish moors and bogs; in summer the soft, pale green, deciduous leaves are conspicuous among the heather. It has been said that the first tender leaves cannot be distinguished from real tea when properly gathered and dried, but it is for the sharp flavoured fruit that blaeberry is best known. The berries are rich in vitamin C and have a healing effect on diarrhoea and dysentery; the addition of a few fruits to blaeberry leaf tea makes a soothing health drink. Collecting the berries from July to September was often left to children, as it can be laborious work searching among heather for the scattered black fruits with their whitish bloom. On a warm summer's day it takes great dedication to collect enough to take home and cook, because it is far too tempting simply to eat the blaeberries as they are found. They are traditionally served in the Highlands stewed in milk, or made into tarts and jellies. Blaeberry jelly mixed with whisky was given to visitors in the eighteenth century.

Wild Strawberry

PARTAN BREE

The large edible crab, or partan, makes a delicious summer soup. Scotland's fisherfolk benefited most from the plentiful daily catch of crab in the days before it was possible to transport them further afield. Now, however, it is possible to buy crab even in inland towns like Aberfeldy, which is fortunate enough to have a fishmonger who makes regular trips to Oban for supplies.

It is always important to use ingredients which are fresh and in perfect condition, and this is particularly vital when preparing shellfish such as lobster, crab and crayfish. It is best to purchase live crab where possible; failing that, establish with the fishmonger selling cooked or dressed crab that it is really fresh. Serve partan bree garnished with mustard cress and with wholemeal bread or rolls.

CROWDIE EGGS

Scotland offers many kinds of eggs besides the usual variety of hens' eggs: duck, turkey, goose, quail and gull - all are fresh and free from the additives used to produce battery hens' eggs and you can taste the difference.

Nowadays scavenging gulls live inland as well as on the coast - the result of more land being used for open refuse tipping. Gulls' eggs are collected on large estates and fetch good prices as a delicacy in markets as far away as London. The eggs of most wild birds are protected (see *Wild Birds and the Law* published by the RSPB) and a licence (from the Scottish Development Department) is required to permit the collecting of gulls' eggs. Most eggs can be transformed with a filling of crowdie and herbs. Crowdie is traditional Scottish cream cheese. Made from warm cow's milk it was once found all over the Highlands of Scotland and often provided the main basis for a meal accompanied by oatcakes or freshly made bread. The whey that was separated from the curds was frequently made into whey oatcakes, warmed before eating.

In the past junket or 'yearned milk' was a useful pudding standby, especially for delicate appetites. Like crowdie, junket is made with warm milk. Rennet is stirred into the milk, flavourings like brandy or vanilla and sugar added, and the mixture allowed to set to be topped with nutmeg and cream if desired. Once set, the junket will 'cry', or separate from the curds, if disturbed.

Crowdie is served with many variations. Spices and herbs such as paprika, black pepper, chopped chives, garlic and nuts can be mixed with the cheese, according to one's taste. The mixture can be served on its own with oatcakes, or with vegetables and eggs to make a more substantial dish like crowdie eggs. Quail eggs, hard boiled in their delicately marked cream-and-brown shells, make a very attractive garnish for dishes like this.

CROWN ROAST OF LAMB AND SKIRLIE

After the battle of Culloden in 1746 Bonnie Prince Charlie went into hiding in many different parts of Scotland. He fled from mansion to hut and cave. One of his many hideouts in the Highlands was a wooden hut built against a mountain cliff of Benalder. It was called the Prince's Cage - an exceedingly good hiding place where he could even light a fire, as the drifting smoke was camouflaged against the grey rock. Macpherson of Breachachy tended to him, bringing daily supplies of food and news of the whereabouts of the Redcoats. At times Macpherson took up baskets of bread, fruit and milk and at others a whole carcass of deer or sheep was flung over his shoulder.

Many Highlanders today still say that the flavour of mutton far excels lamb. It derives its sweet delicious taste from the grazing throughout the seasons on mountain plants and herbs like wild thyme. A gigot of mutton slowly cooked with whole vegetables in a large black pot over a fire was a favourite dish - and hard to beat, oven cooked. Before ovens came into general use, the big black pot hung from the 'swee', an indispensable piece of early kitchen equipment consisting of an metal arm projecting above the fire.

What could have been more fitting than for Macpherson of Breachachy to present two best ends of neck of lamb to the Prince and to cook it for him over the fire on Benalder, serving it shaped in a crown stuffed with oatmeal? Skirlie often accompanied meat and at times was served as a main meal with potatoes. Skirlie, made with the fat off the meat, onions and oatmeal, is the ideal stuffing for a crown roast.

CRANACHAN IN CHOUX

The mid-nineteenth century is still remembered as the time of the clearances when people were forced to leave their homes, many emigrating to America and beyond. Like other emigrants, the Highlanders who sailed to Newfoundland took memories of their homeland and recipes for the dishes they grew up with. Cranachan is one of the recipes they have cherished and make today - with their own variation. Newfoundlanders often hide wrapped silver pieces - silver coins and good-luck charms - in the pudding, just as we do for Christmas pudding. Perhaps they began putting the silver in the cranachan because they could not get ingredients like dried fruit for the more traditional Christmas pudding.

Cranachan is also known as cream crowdie. Soft fruits (raspberries are the classic fruit for cranachan) are stirred into a mixture made with lightly toasted oatmeal and sweetened whipped cream. There are now many variations of this dessert and ice cream is sometimes substituted for the cream. Crowdie mowdie is a more substantial pudding and is made by soaking oatmeal in milk overnight, then steaming it the following day. The traditional cranachan can be served with shortbread or sweet biscuits. Cranachan in choux pastry and coated with white chocolate is extremely good and makes a change from the usual presentation.

TALKING OF SALMON

Neil MacLean

If there is one fish that people associate with Scotland, it must be the salmon. Though, nowadays, the fish they find on their plates is more likely to have been professionally farmed, scientifically cultivated in a cage floating on a loch, than to have recently leapt from one of Scotland's legendary salmon rivers.

I recently fell to reflecting on a salmon dish cooked by one of the world's favourite airlines. 'We only use wild salmon when it is in season,' the executive chef insisted, escorting me round the first class kichen. This seemed highly laudable, until I realised that the dish being made was fish *coulibiac* - using braised rice, mushrooms, eggs and salmon in a pastry case - the whole thing to be reheated and consumed at 33,000 feet where your sense of taste is duller anyway. Could anyone really discern that they were eating wild salmon, I wondered; and does it matter anyway? As a topic of conversation, it seemed a good excuse for lunch.

Good food and lively conversation positively compliment one another. Planning to invite guests to a meal, my first question is: what shall we be eating? (and if I have a say in the matter, it will be fish). You should never leave food to chance, and if I can make sure that one of the people involved is my own choice of chef (in this case, Bruce Sangster) I'm a happy man. And what better company to invite along to discuss the salmon than Claire Macdonald and John Noble?

Claire Macdonald of Macdonald, cookery writer and co-proprietor of Kinloch Lodge on Skye, has written a great deal about salmon and salmon farming. She won't touch farmed salmon if she can avoid it and makes vigorous efforts (so far successful) to keep it from her door. John Noble, chairman of Loch Fyne Oysters, appreciates a good wild salmon as much as Claire does, but as the owner of a salmon farm, he is well placed to play devil's advocate and generally stir the waters.

Chef Bruce Sangster devised a six-course lunch for us in the kitchens at The Murrayshall Hotel in Perthshire and, as five of the six courses featured either wild or farmed salmon, it seemed that we would have a lot to talk about. In my self-appointed role I felt more like a fly on the water than the wall, testing and teasing until I drew out a lively discussion to match the food.

I thought Claire might be easy to bait. Surely, I suggested, there were lots of good things to be said for farmed salmon? But she was feeling conciliatory. 'The best thing to be said for farming is that it makes salmon available to everybody' - then she warmed to her task - 'in the same way as chicken. That used to be a great treat for weekends. Now it is an everyday dish, but of course, it doesn't taste as it did. It is very difficult to find chicken in the shops with any real flavour. Fortunately, with salmon, you can still choose whether you buy farmed or wild in season.'

Claire Macdonald and John Noble with Bruce Sangster and Neil MacLean at The Murrayshall Hotel

John Noble was quick to point out that, without farmed salmon, the wild option would become increasingly scarce. 'There is no doubt that wild salmon is at risk of being overfished, and salmon farming obviously eases pressure on the wild.' 'But at what cost to the environment?' Claire asked. 'The ecological effects from salmon farming seem to me disastrous. It is changing the life on the beds of the lochs and in the rock pools round the coast. We went for a picnic not so long ago, to a place close to a salmon farm, and there was hardly a sea anemone to be found among the rocks.'

The sight of the farms themselves also distresses her. 'Visitors come to Scotland to enjoy the scenery, they see the farms and say, what a shame.' 'Whether salmon farms look bad or good,' John rejoined, 'is to do with where they are sighted. It is the same with caravan parks. However,' he added, 'there should be stricter planning controls over the size and situation of the farms, and this is the responsibility of the Crown Commission.' Claire obviously agreed with this point. 'The whole thing is out of control. There is hardly a waterway that hasn't got a development.'

'Well there are plenty on Loch Fyne,' said John, 'but I wouldn't call them rampant. You can hardly see our farm - which, incidently, employs forty people, many with families!' I had been saving that point for a lull in the conversation - there wasn't one! Claire Macdonald quickly went on to point out that most of the farms are owned by multinational companies who don't employ enough local people. 'But you must include the local downstream related activities,' said John, 'such as smoking the fish and driving the lorries.'

It wasn't an acrimonious discussion. I think it was more what is called a frank exchange of views, but, even so, with those moments of concord and harmony engendered by fine food and wine. We hardly touched on the subject of smoked salmon, agreeing that it would be very hard to tell the difference between a wild and a farmed fish after it had been cured and smoked. I knew from talking to the smokers, however, that they welcome the consistency in size and condition of farmed salmon when they have a lot of fish to prepare. If the flesh is too soft though, or has been badly handled, as can be the case with some farmed fish, it produces a rather mushy smoked salmon that you would rather spread than carve.

As each dish was placed before us by the attentive staff at The Murrayshall Hotel, we sighed with admiration and our thoughts turned to the taste of the salmon and its preparation. 'I would much rather,' John declared, 'eat a top-quality farmed salmon than a wild fish that has been frozen.' That was asking for trouble! 'I wouldn't agree at all,' Claire retorted. 'But the wild salmon must have been frozen properly.' We persuaded her to part with her secret. 'You must gut the fish first, dip it in water, then freeze it for the first time, then dip it in water and freeze it again, until you have developed several layers of ice around the fish.'

Finally they agreed that the best way to cook a good salmon is the least complicated way - either baked simply in the oven with lots of butter, or placed in a cold court-bouillon (John adds a bottle of dry white wine) in a fish kettle or similar vessel, brought gently to a simmer then switched off and allowed to cool.

When Bruce Sangster joined us for dessert he told us that his father used to bring water and vinegar to the boil, slip his salmon in, take it off the heat and eat it cold the next day. As for his own views on the merits of wild and farmed salmon, he was even-handed. 'I use farmed salmon in the early part of the year when I can't get wild. Farmed salmon from Shetland seems to be good. They say that they have stronger currents up there which produce a better fish. If I am doing a mousse or a pâté I'll use farmed salmon, but ideally, for something that needs a bit of texture, I prefer to buy a wild salmon. Whichever you use, it is still a magnificent fish.' Of course he was right. The proof and the pudding had already been eaten.

OYSTERS NOW & THEN
John Noble

'Wha'l o caller oysters' was the street cry of the eighteenth century Edinburgh oyster lassies. A contemporary account describes it 'echoing through the spacious streets of the New Town, though not easily understood, especially by our southern visitors, (it) has a fullness of sound, by no means unpleasant to the ear'. Nor it seems was the lass herself likely to be less attractive than her familiar call since 'under a pea jacket and superabundance of petticoats with which they load themselves' many 'conceal a symmetry of form that might excite the envy of a Duchess'.

Their capacious creels however held no mere dainty Duchess-like load but some 200 lbs (91 kg) weight of oysters 'new drawn frae the Forth'. With this rapid and decorative delivery service direct from Newhaven, the households in the New Town were plentifully supplied with their favourite shell fish delicacy. That oysters were indeed favourites seems clear, for the Ettrick Shepherd in Christopher North's *Noctes Ambrosianae* remarks that 'Embro devours a hunder thoosand every day'.

However the real fun in those days was to be found less in the genteel confines of the New Town than in the oyster cellars of the Old Town like the howff run by the famous and racy hostess Lucky Middlemass. Here in 'laigh' (low) shops the most fashionable people in town mixed with all comers, rich and poor, including Lucky Middlemass's girls to 'regale themselves with raw oysters and porter arranged in huge dishes upon a coarse table' and when the feast got underway 'a thousand remarks and jokes which elsewhere would have been suppressed as improper were here sanctified by the oddity of the scene'.

A convivial and indeed civilised scene and one well known to Burns and Fergusson. The latter wrote verses in praise of much loved oysters, though for all his healthy oyster eating, which modern medicine would endorse, Fergusson died at the early age of twenty four:

Come prie, frail man! for gin thou art sick,
The oyster is a rare cathartic,
As ever doctor patient gart lick
To cure his ails;
Whether you hae the head or heart-ake
It ay prevails

Eighteenth century Edinburgh oyster lassie. Scots need neither title nor fortune to enjoy oysters nowadays

Right through the nineteenth century oysters were abundant and cheap. Some 1000 million were eaten in Britain only one hundred years ago. Then a combination of pollution and a variety of diseases and parasites, some from the United States, devastated the oyster beds. It is doubtful whether even one oyster bed exists today in the once prolific Firth of Forth. Native oysters, *Ostrea Edulis*, have become very scarce and exceedingly expensive. A wealthy merchant banker might buy a dozen at Wilton's in Jermyn Street, St James's, for an important client but the ordinary mortal fights shy of such an expenditure. Some would claim that he or she had lost the taste for them. Yet all is not dark and gloomy on the supply front for the aspirant oyster lover anxious to relive the halcyon days of old.

'Westward look and land lies bright' or to be rather more specific, there are stretches of foreshore on the West Coast of Scotland not only ideal for growing oysters but now actually growing them in some quantity in a number of locations.

Some ten years ago Andrew Lane, then a manager of a salmon farm at the head of Loch Fyne, startled me by suggesting farming oysters on the stretch of foreshore belonging to the Ardkinglas Estate. Though I knew our beaches were littered with old oyster shells of unknown antiquity I had never seen a live survivor. My humble war work as a six or seven year old lad was to pound up oyster shells to feed to the hens. The possibility of oysters in the Loch again seemed curious and exciting.

Andrew Lane and I anxiously experimented. We placed a stock of about six plastic trays containing seed oysters half way down the beach in the pure, fertile waters of the loch. The small sixpenny sized oysters lived and perceptibly grew, notwithstanding our daily baleful inspections. So an oyster growing enterprise was born. We later discovered that our pilot scheme had, in fact, a very poor chance of survival because our experimental trays were positioned where they were vulnerable to layers of cold, fresh water. It was the purest good fortune that all the seed oysters did not perish and with them the concept of an oyster farm!

Now, after some ten years and many 'slips twixt the shell and the lip', a solid commercial enterprise has been established. We ourselves approach sales of one million oysters per year of the *Gigas* variety and there are other farms emerging in the West Highlands and Islands. When you consider that the coastline of Argyll is longer than the entire coastline of France without taking into consideration the hundreds of miles of coast on the remaining Highland West Coast and Islands, it is easy to understand that an enormous production of oysters is possible in the Highlands.

The French, after all, eat some 1300 million oysters per year, almost all home produced (*huitres creuses - Gigas*) from a far smaller growing area than we have in Scotland. In the UK we eat only around six million per year; an amount we could nearly satisfy from the Ardkinglas foreshore. Indeed there are indications that a revolution in eating is underway and that the old Scottish predilection for this mollusc lurk below only a superficial unfamiliarity. A young lad of about ten visited our stand at the Royal Highland Show a year or two ago. He shut his eyes tightly to swallow his first oyster, beamed with relief when the experiment was over and consumed eight more in rapid succession, in a manner which would not have shamed a seasoned French *escallier* (oyster-seller). At the 1988 Edinburgh International Festival a reception was held at the National Galleries of Scotland for some 800 - 900 people. The 3000 oysters we sent for the event vanished almost too rapidly, 'like snow off a dyke', confounding the doubters. At our Oyster Bar and shop at the head of Loch Fyne some 3000 oysters per week are used in the busy season. A tremendous cross section of people sit down at the 'coarse' wooden table to enjoy oysters and wines though we lack certain other amenities that the old howffs used to provide! It seems a renaissance in oyster eating 'is coming yet for a' that'.

An anonymous French poet, with possibly a better sense of values than sense of poetry, once wrote:

> *Avec les huitres*
> *Que le Chablis est excellent*
> *Je donerai fortune et titre*
> *Pour m'enivrer de ce vin blanc*
> *Avec les huitres*

Lucky Middlemass would drink to that sentiment. She always put a good ashet of oysters before considerations of fortune and titles. In any case, thanks to West Coast production, you now need neither title nor fortune to enjoy oysters.

AUTUMN CHEFS

MARK SALTER

breasts of pigeon wrapped
in brussels sprout leaves
with wild rice pancakes
loin of rabbit wrapped in schüpfnüdeln
with a port wine sauce
compote of leeks with oranges
glazed apple pancakes
with glenlivet, oatmeal & honey ice cream
poppy seed parfait with poached pear &
citrus fruit mousse & bramble sauce

GRAHAM NEWBOULD

glazed loch linnhe prawns
with garlic & herb butter
grilled breast of woodpigeon
with warm cumberland sauce
roast saddle of roe deer
with apple purée & rosemary sauce
tears of dark chocolate with whisky mousse

HELEN BROUGHTON

roast pheasant with celery & walnut stuffing
scots potatoes

HARVEST AT HOME

spiced plums
pears in red wine
hallowe'en stew
pumpkin pie

FARE FOR FEASTING

boletus burgers
rowan jelly
rosehip syrup
elderberry cordial

TRADITIONAL MENU

chanterelle soup
mussels whisky cream
game pie
blaeberry pancakes

*Chanterelles and ceps
gathered in a Perthshire
wood by chef Mark Salter*

AUTUMN CHEFS

Neil MacLean

In autumn, thoughts of the natural Scottish larder turn to game. One of the few areas of the world that shares our wealth of wild game is the Black Forest, and **Mark Salter** used to work in Baden Baden. Now, as chef at Cromlix House, Mark has access to the best ingredients that Scotland can produce, and he will often put ideas brought back from Germany into practice.

For example, he likes to prepare rabbit wrapped in a traditional German *schüpfnüdeln* paste. The rabbits, like so much of the game he cooks, come from the Cromlix House estate. For a while, pigeon was out of fashion, but it is making a welcome return and Mark likes to prepare it with a veal and pistachio nut stuffing. Pheasant he cooks with morels and fresh herbs or with a bread and *foie gras* stuffing.

Mark grew up in a small village near Sudbury, studied at Colchester College, and continued his culinary education in Switzerland, Germany and the Hotel de Cap between Nice and Cannes. He describes his cooking as 'classic modern cuisine', but one difference between his presentation of a dish and most of his contemporaries is that he likes to include the vegetables on the main plate. 'I don't think you get a full appreciation of your meal when it is on two separate plates - I prefer to involve the colour of the vegetables with the meat or fish.'

He grows many of the vegetables he uses himself. Celeriac is particularly good in autumn and goes very well with game. He makes, for example, a timbale of carrot and celeriac to serve with roe deer. He grows fruit in the estate greenhouse - figs to accompany a quail and roe deer terrine served with apricot and ginger sauce. Rowanberries, growing near the hotel, are picked to make jam with orange muscat wine. From early autumn until the first chill frosts, Mark derives tremendous pleasure from combing the undergrowth of a nearby copse for ceps and chanterelles.

That is how chef **Graham Newbould**, too, would choose to spend his day off during the mushroom season. Roaming the hills and glens around Fort William, he has come to know a special place for each wild mushroom, Achnacarry for chanterelle, Glen Nevis for white *pleurotte*, Onich for cep and Clunes for *pied de mouton*. These he takes to Inverlochy Castle to make two of his specialities - a *feuillette* of wild mushrooms and wild mushroom broth with mussels.

It is a long way from Wakefield to Fort William. It is a long way from a general catering course to a Michelin star, and Graham Newbould's route has taken him through London's Connaught Hotel, the kitchens at Buckingham Palace and, before coming to Inverlochy Castle, he was Royal Chef at Kensington Palace. On several occasions he cooked for the Royal Family on the Balmoral Estate and found there the freshest of local produce. The range of game he prepared there has influenced the menus he creates at Inverlochy Castle.

He prefers to cook roe deer rather than venison and only uses the eye of the meat, which he will marinate in wine for two days, before it is cooked and served with a rosemary sauce and apple purée. Apple goes very well with roe deer and rosemary is available throughout the winter in his garden, along with bay leaves, and, earlier in the year, chervil, dill and other herbs.

He also buys partridge and grouse, snipe, woodcock and wild duck. 'Wild duck need careful cooking as they must be served pink or rare', says Graham, who likes to accompany the dish with a fruit-based sauce or braised cabbage. Forget the horrors of school-dinner cabbage. Graham Newbould cooks his for three hours - with ham hocks, knuckle of veal and a *mirepoix* of vegetables for this and for his chartreuse of grouse.

In Fort William, he is well placed for deliveries of West Coast fish and shellfish. Much of the seafood prepared at Inverlochy Castle comes through Simon McDonald of Glenuig. Graham might steam the lobsters and serve them with a champagne and chive sauce and serve crabs cold with a

Graham Newbould (left) creates dishes which are influenced by the fresh local produce and game he used when he cooked for the Royal Family at Balmoral. Mark Salter (right) has access to the best ingredients in Scotland's natural larder and describes his cooking as 'classic modern cuisine'

pink grapefruit salad. Queen scallops come from Glenborrodale, king scallops arrive daily from Mallaig, and prawns (with which he makes a mouthwatering garlic and herb butter) come from Loch Linnhe.

Graham Newbould is particularly renowned for his marvellous desserts. Roasted strawberries with a grapefruit sorbet demonstrates his original and often inspired use of produce, while tears of bitter chocolate filled with a whisky mousse are very comforting when you find the wettest place in Britain living up to its reputation.

HARVEST AT HOME
Kirsty Burrell

Autumn is the most hardworking, but satisfying, time of year in the kitchen. Gluts in the vegetable garden, orchard and hedgerow seem daunting at first and my squirrel instinct - a relic, perhaps, of times when housewives had to bottle, salt and preserve in the season of plenty to see their families through the season of scarcity - compels me to slave; but nothing beats the virtuous feeling inspired by neatly labelled freezer cartons and jars of jams, jellies and pickles, glowing 'like good deeds in a naughty world'.

So the big brass jelly pan bubbles, the jelly bag drip-drips, the wooden spoons are all purple and every surface in the kitchen is sticky; saucers sit about with scummy, fruity blobs ('is it setting?') and the whole house smells of fruit and burnt sugar.

Brambles make the best-flavoured jelly. They also freeze well for winter puddings - bramble and apple tarts, cranachan made with toasted oatmeal and greek-style yogurt. The slightly tart jelly made from rowan berries is the traditional accompaniment to game. I also use it in glazes and sauces where redcurrant jelly is suggested. The berries should be picked after the first frost. I add some apples to help it set. Apple jellies with herbs are useful for serving with meat. A bunch of the required herb (thyme, tarragon, mint) should be boiled with the apples, then the fresh herbs are put into the jars just before filling. Attractively packaged, all these things make presents for holiday visiting or Christmas giving.

This is the time to make chutney - plum, pear or apple - to eat with the stilton or baked ham at Christmas. I also make whole spiced plums, plums and brandy for the festive entertaining season and pears in red wine which freeze well. If you have a fruit tree in the garden you need to collect a file of recipes for dealing with its progeny.

Sloes, like rowans, should be gathered after the first frosts. Sloe gin is easy to make and has a wonderful rich colour and taste, the tart flavour of the berries coming through the sweetness. Damson gin is also very good. Damsons are underestimated.

Pickles and preserves 'glowing like good deeds in a naughty world'

Their little stones are a pest - there always seems to be so many of them - but the fruit makes the most delicious, unusual purple fools and ice-creams.

It is worth putting some apple purée in the freezer for sauces to go with roast pork. Whole apples, cored and stuffed with mincemeat (this is the time to make mincemeat for Christmas pies) wrapped in pastry and decorated with pastry leaves, can be stored in the freezer and make a filling pudding after a meal of soup, bread and cheese.

My cooking tends to get heartier with the first frosts. The crisp salads and refreshing sorbets of summer give way to soups, stews and fruit crumbles. Soup can be made from almost any vegetable, cooked in chicken stock and puréed with the addition of a handful of rice, pearl barley or some broken pasta. Soup freezes very successfully, so if you make an enormous potful the family does not have to eat the same thing every day for a week. Scotland has a tradition of good nourishing soups like cock-a-leekie, kail brose, partan bree and cullen skink. Soups made with dried pulses - lentils, split peas or the broth mix containing dried pulses and herbs which you buy in most grocers need the stronger taste of stock. Scottish butchers sell ham shanks or smokey ham ribs for this purpose.

Venison used to be the perogative of crowned heads and aristocracy. Nowadays some of them are glad to sell it to us commoners, and with the advent of deer farming it has come down in price. I can remember, as a child, reading about Robin Hood and his Merry Men feasting on venison stew, and imagining what it might taste like, long before I had the opportunity to eat the real thing. It was not a disappointment.

For a grand occasion, I bake venison in a pastry case (which has the added advantage of conserving the juices, otherwise the meat can be a bit dry). A big venison stew, with a heap of baked potatoes, is an expandable feast for a hungry crowd. At a humbler level, stalkers' pie - the venison version of shepherds' pie, or a venison sausage roll, would make good supper dishes.

The big autumn celebration in Scotland is Hallowe'en. I love it - second only to Christmas. The children decorate the dining room with dangling witches and ghosts and stick wicked faces on the windows. There is much frantic preparation of costumes and rehearsing of songs and poems for guising. I put huge bowls of apples, satsumas and nuts (and some 10p pieces!) in the hall ready for the guisers. Excited little witches and wizards dook for apples swirling in the washing-up bowl. I hang doughnuts dripping with treacle from a washing-line (scones are traditional but doughnuts are easier to string-up) to eat with hands behind the back.

Until recently, we stuck to the traditional Scottish 'tumshie' - a turnip hollowed out and carved with a frightening face and a candle set inside. But I must confess that (like many Scots, judging from the piles of pumpkins in every corner shop) we have gone over to the American-style pumpkin lantern. It is much easier to hollow-out and prettier, although I do miss that funny smell of burning turnip which evokes memories of childhood hallowe'ens.

Above: harvest loaves with ancient origins are made each autumn by Ken Adamson in his Pittenweem bakery. Left: harvest stook with mouse; centre: five loaves and fishes; right: cornucopia with coloured marzipan fruits
Below: pumpkins, fast gaining ground over the Scottish 'tumshie' for Hallowe'en lanterns, provide the basic ingredient of pumpkin stew and pumpkin pie

FARE FOR FEASTING

Tess Darwin

In early autumn nature provides a feast for all, and ever since farming began, once the labour of harvest was over it was a time to celebrate and enjoy the unaccustomed abundance of food, with not just quantity but variety making these the most bountiful months of the year.

Many wild fruits were gathered, to eat fresh or to preserve for the long winter months ahead. There were **blackberries**, *smeuran* or *an druis beannaichte*, the blessed bramble (the leaves of which make a soothing poultice for burns - useful to know in the jam-making season). The closely-related cloudberries (known by a variety of names in Scotland, such as averins, fintocks, knotberries and noops) are small orange fruits with large segments. This is a low, creeping herb of mountains and upland bogs - cloudy places, hence the name. It has soft, downy leaves and does not have the sharp thorns that can make brambling painful. Although not very common, where cloudberries occur they are usually in sufficient quantities to make picking worthwhile. They are juicy and flavoursome when ripe, and used to be greatly prized as a dessert.

Another low, creeping plant with edible fruits is the **dwarf cornel**, which is in the dogwood family. It is fairly common in the central Highlands and southern Scotland, but does not occur on the islands. The berries, like small, shiny raspberries, are sweet but not as fruity as brambles; they were reputed to create a great appetite, but maybe this was just because folk could never find enough of them to feel satisfied!

The beautiful **rowan** trees bear their bright red clusters of berries from September right through the winter, providing an important source of food for birds. Most old Scottish houses have a rowan tree nearby, because it was believed to provide powerful protection against evil and enchantment. The berries are usually at their best in October when fully ripe; later they go squashy. They have long been used for making wine, and also for distilling a very potent spirit. Nowadays they are more

Cloudberry

Loaves and fishes at Adamson's bakery

commonly made into rowan jelly, the traditional accompaniment to venison and grouse.

Elderberries are usually abundant in autumn, and the masses of luscious black fruits are irresistible. They are best known for making cordial and wine with proven medicinal qualities, particularly beneficial for the winter ailments of coughs, colds and other chest troubles. Mulled elderberry wine is an unsurpassed tonic after a damp day in the hills. The berries can be served in pies (adding apples for bulk and to soak up the juice), and traditionally were dried for use like raisins in baking.

In early autumn, before the leaves begin to turn, and later in the year when trees and shrubs are bare, **rosehips** in the hedgerows provide delightful splashes of colour. They have been used for drinks, desserts and jam for many generations, and contain more vitamin C than almost anything else we know - about twenty times as much as the same weight of oranges. Rosehip tea can be bought in many shops these days, and is an excellent drink throughout the year, but picking fresh rosehips on a golden day is an activity not to be missed. They are best when fully ripe and after the first frost, usually around early October.

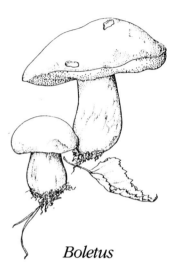

Boletus

Perhaps because they are so ephemeral, wild mushrooms are one of autumn's greatest delights, yet they are now very little known in Scotland compared to mainland Europe and Scandinavia. It is right to be extremely cautious when collecting wild mushrooms, because some are deadly poisonous, but it seems a great shame to miss out altogether on the subtle flavours and varied textures of the many edible types when accurate identification is possible with the help of a good field guide.

Dwarf Cornel

Chanterelles are a good type to start with, because they are unlikely to be confused with any poisonous variety, and are rarely eaten by the maggots which often infest other kinds. Chanterelles grow in woodland, particularly under pine, birch and beech, from August until winter frosts begin. They have both the colour and fragrance of fresh apricots, with gills that run down the stem. They can be gently stewed in milk or sauteed in

68

butter, requiring longer cooking than cultivated mushrooms to tenderise them and enhance the delicate flavour. They are excellent served in an omelette or casserole.

Another unmistakable type of mushroom with no poisonous look-alikes is the **puff-ball**. Many species are good to eat while young and white, when they are very conspicuous whether growing in woods or grassland, but old specimens should be left well alone. They do not require peeling, but sliced thinly can be used like cultivated mushrooms. People living on Orkney in the Stone Age are known to have collected puff-balls, although only mature specimens have been found, suggesting they were used medicinally (to staunch bleeding) rather than as food.

Boletus mushrooms, also known as ceps, do not have gills beneath the cap, but appear to be filled with sponge, making them easy to distinguish from other kinds. They grow throughout the autumn near trees (but not in dense shade), and many ceps are edible; any tinged with red or purple on the pores or stem should be avoided, and all specimens should be checked for unwanted wildlife before adding to the cooking pan! One of the most popular fungi in earlier times, it was simply known as the edible boletus or penny-bun, because that is just what it looks like. It has a smooth, dry chestnut-coloured cap 2-8 inches (5-20 cm) across; the spongy area is white when young, and is best eaten then before it turns yellowish. In older specimens it should be scooped out with a spoon before cooking; they are best gently fried rather than grilled, and can be dried for later use.

Chanterelle

CHANTERELLE (OR WILD MUSHROOM) SOUP

We have a new kind of 'poacher' searching through the fields and woods - for mushrooms and fungi - as more and more people become aware of their value. There are many different kinds in Scotland, each with an individual flavour, but care and knowledge is required, of course, in selecting non-poisonous varieties.

Chanterelles have recently become one of the most popular and sought-after wild mushroooms both in this country and on the continent. They are usually found under birch or beech trees, often hidden in the moss. Their distinctive odour is reminiscent of dried apricots and their yellow-gold colour makes them stand out in the undergrowth. They can transform the whole dish - soup, casseroles or grill - to which they are added.

Chanterelle soup is one of the best soups I know; it has a rich creamy consistency and a flavour which is unique. It can be made in the same way as a cream of mushroom soup.

In the past we have, perhaps, been over canny; our fields and undergrowth are full of edible fungi, and there is no reason why we, like our European neighbours, cannot learn the basic rules for avoiding the poisonous varieties. But, at last, we are starting to appreciate their true value.

MUSSELS WHISKY CREAM

Scotland produces large quantities of mussels and in former days they were an everyday food which people enjoyed. The town of Musselburgh, near Edinburgh, was renowned for the quality and quantity of mussels harvested from the Firth of Forth. Some cooks now prefer to buy farmed mussels which have the advantage of being virtually free from barnacles and easy to prepare.

There are two main varieties of mussels, the large ones, known in Gaelic as the *clabach dubh* ('black mouth'), and the smaller ones. Some say that the smaller ones have a more delicate flavour but I find the *clabach dubh* equally good. In the course of preparation it is important to remove the 'beards'. These are threads on the shells which enable the mussels to cling to the rocks; not even the turbulent seas can dislodge them. This done, the shells should be washed and scrubbed, if necessary. Discard open mussels and any which fail to open when cooked.

Like wild mushrooms and game, mussels, underrated until recently, are are becoming a popular food again. Economical and nourishing, they can form the basis of superb yet simple dishes.

GAME PIE

Game pie was an ideal dish to make when the gamekeeper or man of the house came back from the hill with his mixed bag of game which might include grouse, partridge, pigeon and other creatures of the wild. Nowadays, even good city butchers keep a supply of game in season, making it much more widely available than ever before.

Game pies are served both hot and cold; when cold a delicious jelly from the cooking juices sets over the meat. Sometimes, stock and gelatine are poured into a small hole in the pie crust to add to the jelly around the meats. These pies have much thicker pastry than fruit pies and were at times quite ornate, with pastry decorations of leaves and other embellishments. The Highlanders were very reliant on game, and although they did not realise it at the time, they had a healthy diet; game is nourishing and low in cholesterol. But 'feast or famine' rang true at times of the year when game, and other sources of protein, ran short. Then, it was common practice for cattle drovers, finding themselves a long way from food, to make a nick in a cow's neck, allow blood to collect in a bowl and then mix it with oatmeal - the likely origin of black pudding.

BLAEBERRY PANCAKES

The blaeberry is also known as the bilberry, and was called a variety of local names as well. The small round purple berries are found among the heaths and heathers on the moors. Because the fruit is so succulent it needs very little water in its cooking.

All traditional Scottish kitchens had a girdle which was constantly in use for making scones and pancakes. There was a large variety, soda scones, fruit scones, drop scones and saucer pancakes. The Scottish crumpet or girdle cake is common today and made fairly thin so that it can be rolled up. Except in poor households, they were always on the tea table or breakfast table. Fruit or savoury filling was sometimes piled on top of a large pancake, folded over and baked in the oven. Stuffed pancakes are delicious with both savoury and sweet fillings and blaeberries give them a superb sharp flavour. The fruit can either be cooked or folded into sugar and whipped cream.

Scotland still has some of the wildest landscapes in Europe. Intensive farming methods and agricultural policies of other countries have helped to make it so, and it is a curious coincidence that one of the principal reasons for the sudden popularity of grouse shooting in the early years of the nineteenth century stemmed from improved methods of farming in England. Reduction of truly wild sport was a consequence of marginal land being brought into cereal production, so shooting men looked towards the Scottish grouse moors for their autumn holiday.

The mystique of the red grouse, and the enthusiasm with which it is pursued, dates from that time. A desire for greater leisure in peaceful surroundings followed the end of the long Napoleonic Wars. At the same time refinements to firearms, in terms of size, weight and accuracy, increased the attraction of shooting birds on the wing. Added to that, the revolution in transport made Scotland easily accessible. By the 1830s the coach journey from London to Edinburgh took only forty-two hours, and a decade later the arrival of the railways enabled travellers to reach Scotland much more quickly. The number of people taking up shooting rose dramatically.

The unique landscape in which the red grouse lives, allied to the fact that it is resident only in the British Isles and nowhere else in the world, combine to give it unrivalled glamour. As early as 1826 Emily Eden wrote critically of a suitor who had failed to propose to a lady and, instead, had gone off to the moors. 'Probably, in the way men usually do, he settled that though he could propose any day, he could go out grouse-shooting only on the Twelfth, and while the grouse might grow wild she would remain tame, so that he had better attend to the grouse first and woo the lady later.'

The moors of northern England have consistently yielded larger bags than Scotland, but the grouse has always been more associated with the Scottish hills and glens where the English ruling classes gathered for their holidays. In the early Victorian era it was a bachelor expedition to rude accommodation in a shepherd's bothy or a primitively furnished and heated lodge. But as demand for Scottish sport grew, rents were pushed up and landowners could afford to build luxurious lodges for their tenants.

The provision of homely comforts soon attracted family parties to migrate north for a holiday lasting several weeks. Scottish estates offered advantages which England could not match - deer-stalking with a variety of rough shooting and fishing. Salmon and trout fishing appealed to the ladies, and while they were not expected to shoot, they were encouraged to fish and took to it with enthusiasm.

The pattern of Scottish sport remained generally unaltered until the Second World War. Landowners either retained sport on their estates for their own use, or let them to one tenant for the season or, sometimes, for a period of years. Thus the less wealthy, who wanted an occasional modest day's shooting, were denied it. Happily, that system has changed, and landlords are prepared to let shooting for short periods, even a single day, to those who seek it. The inflated prices of the nineteenth century no longer exist and, contrary to popular belief, a day of 'walked-up' grouse is within the pocket of more people than ever. The bag of say, ten brace for a party of four guns will cost approximately £100 for each person. For a day that will long be remembered, in unparalleled scenery far from the cares of business, some people consider that is not a high price to pay.

The sportsman is likely to take home with him, as part of the deal, a brace of grouse, and young birds should be selected if sufficient are shot. The ability to distinguish between young and old birds is important. Purely on outward appearance no test is infallible. Indeed, the most reliable guide to age is to compare the shape of the two outer primary wing feathers with the rest. If they all have similarly rounded tips it is an old bird, but if the tips

are pointed, clearly differing in shape from the others, the bird is young.

The older birds also have merit, so should not be discounted. The common advice that they should be consigned to the casserole is sound, but slowly roasted they can be as tender as their off-spring and they retain the inimitable, and intense, flavour of the heather.

How long birds should be hung is a matter of personal taste, but I do not share the view that a bird plucked warm may be eaten the day it is killed. To give them tenderness young grouse should be hung for three days and old birds for five or six. That is long enough for meat which is naturally strong in flavour, though opinions differ. Professor George Saintsbury, the great Victorian writer on food and wine, said that a friend of his kept a supply of grouse hanging till he could accompany them with salmon caught in a river (which was by no means early in the year) and he never found better tasting birds.

To retain moisture and flavour, all birds should be hung in feather until cooked. After plucking and drawing, the liver should be left inside if the grouse is to be roasted. To roast, wrap the bird in bacon and place on a piece of toast (20 minutes for each pound (half kilo) in weight). The toast, which is brought to the table with the bird on it, will have absorbed the juices from the liver and the bacon in the cooking.

The unique Scottish landscape is the favourite haunt of the red grouse .
Author and hotel owner Ronald Eden was practically born on the moors above Cromlix.
Left: 11-year-old labrador, Jill , brings in the bag

TALKING OF GAME

Neil MacLean

It is unusual to find a game dealer who is also a cordon bleu cook with her own establishment, so Helen Broughton's Stirlingshire restaurant was my first choice for an autumn game lunch. Our guests were Ronald Eden, owner of nearby Cromlix House and its estates, who knows as much about game as anybody (practically born on the moors, he bagged his first grouse by the age of nine); and Damaris Fletcher, who comes from New England and runs a deer farm at Thornhill with her husband.

Before we tucked in to Helen's tempting looking pigeon breast glazed with port we raised our glasses, appropriately filled with *Canard Duchene,*

was a need to re-define 'game' in the light of recent changes in production methods and eating habits. With an exquisite rabbit *mirabelle* before us (fillet of rabbit with marjoram and bacon stuffing, wrapped in sorrel, baked in pastry and served with a *mirabelle* sauce) enhanced by a delectable *Fleurie,* we all agreed that game animals were those that were traditionally killed for sport, regardless of how they are now raised. And we happily moved on to consider quail and guinea fowl.

There was a case in point. Quail is considered game, without a doubt. And yet the only place it is found wild these days is Africa. Distracted by the

Chef patron, Helen Broughton (left) with Ronald Eden and Damaris Fletcher at Neil MacLean's game lunch

and mulled over the all-important question: What, precisely, is game? There was pigeon in front of us, but I had never been sure how to categorise pigeon. Despite its 'renaissance' on top class menus in Scotland - did it count as game? 'If you shot one in Trafalgar Square it might not,' teased Damaris. Ronald thought that, strictly speaking, pigeon was not defined as game, which tended to be seasonal.

Then we considered another angle: does game count as game because it isn't a farmed animal? 'But I, like most venison producers, think of farmed deer as game,' said Damaris. 'Besides,' added Ronald, 'venison has been farmed since time immemorial.' It was generally agreed that there

appearance of a delectable pot roast shoulder of venison (venison slowly roasted on a bed of vegetables with juniper, thyme and orange, served with a sauce based on the juices and puréed vegetables) the discussion quickly got down to brass tacks. On the subject of deer, it is interesting that Broughton's only serves red deer, whereas Cromlix House serves roe. It is literally a matter of taste. 'A lot of people will not eat rich meat,' said Helen, 'so my menu may have red deer on it, but there will be several other options.' But I was a little surprised that the restaurants don't offer both types of deer, because as Helen says, 'the difference in taste is as marked as that of beef and lamb'.

Damaris Fletcher raises red deer as breeding animals which are sold on to farmers in the south of England, perhaps, who produce for outlets like Sainsbury's. 'It's impossible to farm roe deer, which are solitary, woodland animals, and we don't have many fallow deer in Scotland.' Apparently, it's very difficult to discern any difference in taste between farmed and wild deer - age is the most important factor when considering the taste of venison. 'If you get one that has been shot when gobbling up your neighbour's barley - if it is young it will be the most delicious beast in the world,' said Damaris, 'but if it is old and it was just shot last week in the middle of the rut it will be disgusting.'

Experiments in New Zealand where deer farming is big business have also shown that what a deer eats has less impact on its taste than its age and how it was killed. 'I want to believe that if it eats nothing but blaeberries and apples and a nice bit of grass it will taste better, but it doesn't,' Helen concurred. 'Age is far more important.' Damaris and Ronald agreed and stressed that how venison is killed is also important, since bad handling at that stage changes the acidity or PH factor in the animal's chemistry.

It seems certain that there will be more and more farmed venison on the market as the meat becomes increasingly popular. 'And, whether you consider them game or not, pigeons too,' said Helen, adding that if pigeon and venison appear on Broughton's menu they sell out right away. We drank a toast to food writers like Nichola Fletcher (a friend of, but not a relation of Damaris's family) who have done much to interest the public in cooking and sampling game.

Then our fine *Amarone Recioto Della Valpolicella* led to a romantic reverie on old methods of rearing pigeon. 'Initially they were kept within castles and later moved out in the square stone buildings in the middle of fields.' 'Doocots,' someone interjected. 'Pigeons would lay their eggs. When these hatched, the squabs' feet - when large enough - would be tied to a ledge and the mother pigeons would keep coming back to feed them. The young pigeons would then get bigger and bigger and bigger - nice and plump for the winter meat.' And we turned once more to rabbit - and hare.

Even more than between red deer and roe deer, there is a marked difference in taste between rabbit and hare. There was general agreement that hare was one of the most delicious meats you can eat, and Ronald Eden ventured his opinion that a blue hare has a much finer taste than a brown hare. As far as cooking is concerned, however, rabbit and hare require similar treatment - they are both very dry meats. 'Like most game, they require nurturing,' said Helen, 'with the help of a fatty meat like bacon.'

Hare, like venison and pigeon, also benefits from the addition of a certain amount of sweetness in the cooking - perhaps from sweet jelly or port. 'It seems to bring out the flavour of the food.' said Helen. She prefers elderberry to rowan jelly, finding the latter rather 'wairch' (somewhat bitter), but she also makes crab apple jelly and hedgerow jelly (which includes almost anything edible from the hedgerows - blackberries, elderberries, rosehips).

Tradition still plays a very important part in the cooking and presentation of game. 'When I first came to Scotland,' said Damaris, 'I thought that bread sauce and breadcrumbs were the most disgusting things in the world. But now I do believe that these traditional accompaniments are wonderful.' Game chips are also a must with grouse and pheasant - a packet of potato crisps will not do instead. 'You should always cook a toast under grouse and serve it with the dish,' said Ronald. 'Sometimes with pheasant and partridge too; the bread helps to digest rich food,' Helen added.

She warmed to the subject of other accompaniments. 'Watercress goes well with game as do any vegetables that are moist, particularly red cabbage.' And you should always eat my Scotch potatoes with venison!' We wheedled the recipe out of her. First thinly slice some potatoes, dip them in an egg wash, roll them in flour then a medium oatmeal and deep fry them. She was right - they were delicious. But the best accompaniment of all turned out to be the conversation and we all agreed that game is among the healthiest and most delicious of all foods from the natural larder.

Scotland enjoys a well-deserved international reputation for the quality of its meat. As a country, we are rolling in fine permanent pasture, the rich green grass which helps to give our meat its special character and flavour. Our traditional native breeds, such as Aberdeen Angus, make for tasty eating, and this unique combination of Scottish 'breed and feed' provides us with meat which is worthy raw material for any cook or chef, whether at home or in a restaurant or hotel.

But we cannot allow ourselves to become too blase. Scottish farmers have been under pressure in the recent past to compete with specialist meat producers. Continental breeds, such as the Limosin and Charollais, were introduced into this country because of their ability to gain weight fast but without too much fat. As a result the meat from these animals does not have the flavour of our native breeds. We have shown ourselves to be as gullible as anyone else in the hands of chemical companies who told us that growth promoters and routine antibiotics in animal feedstuffs would guarantee high yield and bigger profits.

As a result, a growing consumer lobby has become disenchanted with red meat, and we are only now beginning to see the realisation dawning among our meat producers that a return to traditional, natural rearing is the key to long term success.

Encouragingly, we have seen the arrival of the butchers 'Q' Guild, an association of butchers who seek out and consciously promote natural, flavoursome meat in preference to the quickly reared variety. Some of our meat wholesalers have evolved a new 'specially selected' quality mark to delineate their produce from the now meaningless 'Scotch' tag, which had been too loosely used, sometimes to cover meat which did not even originate in Scotland.

All over the country, small producers with an interest in natural meat are springing up. Their animals will graze and roam for most of the summer and are left together in family groups for much longer. No growth enhancers or other additives are given to them. They reach their weight having fed on grass, and in winter, supplements of hay, silage and barley. There is even now strictly organic meat, from animals reared on pure pastures, free from herbicides and pesticides and their attendant chemical residues. Good news for our own health and that of the countryside!

The challenge for the interested cook or chef is to find a good source for meat of quality. Supermarket meat is often an unknown quantity since so little information is provided on the pre-pack label. Go instead to your best local butcher and strike up a conversation with him. Ask him where he buys his meat and how he assesses its quality. Some butchers buy at auction markets and know which farms the animals come from. They then arrange the slaughtering and delivery themselves. Others buy direct from the slaughterhouse or meat processor. How long does he hang his meat? A dependable butcher will allow at least fourteen days, even though the carcass loses weight, therefore monetary value and his cash flow suffers while the meat matures. The less quality-conscious and profit minded butcher will prefer to sell what he buys within days of it coming to the shop to get a quick return on his investment. Gauge your butcher's interest and pride in what he sells, and look to him for guidance in judging what cuts of meat to use, as well as a willingness to butcher meat according to your chosen recipe. A good butcher will always be prepared to answer your questions and value your trade as a discerning customer.

Yet while it should prove relatively straightforward to locate a quality butcher in Scotland who can supply you with fine raw ingredients, the same cannot be said of our meat products. Historically, Scotland has produced some special ones; our famous haggis, mealy puddings, mutton pies, the Hogmanay favourite - steak pie, the original ploughman's lunch and Forfar bridies.

Rack of spring lamb ready for the oven. Small producers with an interest in natural meat are springing up everywhere. A unique combination of Scottish 'breed and feed' gives our best meat its special character and flavour

But, as anyone who has experience of Scottish institutional catering will know all too well, so many of these traditional favourites have become poor unhealthy shadows of their noble ancestors. The day-glo pink 'Lorne' sausage and leaden, fat-saturated meat pie, so basic to most butchers' shops and larger stores, is testimony to the fact that Scots are still remarkably unaware when it comes to assessing the quality and healthiness of prepared foods.

However, things are improving in this respect also. More butchers are responding to the call for meat products of integrity. Really well made traditional butchers' sausages with a high percentage of meat and a minimum of additives are making a comeback. One can even, with a little dedication, track down authentic Ayrshire bacon, a product which cooks to a delightful degree of crispness without exuding the tell-tale watery white liquid of its mass-produced counterpart.

The butchers 'Q' Guild has focused on the generally low standard of 'charcuterie', and each year holds a competition after which prize-winning recipes for pates, sausages, pies, and, most importantly, proper spices and seasonings, are circulated and shared among all members. All this activity bodes well for the future rediscovery of quality meat products in Scotland.

We can take advantage of the excellent value that our meat represents - even the more pricey cuts such as sirloin of beef or loin of lamb currently offer tremendous *rapport qualite prix* (value for money). The time is ripe for a return to enjoying quality meat as part of a good mixed diet.

WINTER CHEFS

BILL GIBB

fillet of lemon sole with chive & scampi mousse
& crayfish sauce & tender young leeks
marinated beef fillet with wild rice timbales
& woodland mushroom port wine sauce
almond cookie basket
filled with drambuie ice cream

PETER JUKES

turnip & pine kernel soup
mushrooms stuffed with haggis
quail with pistachio & herb stuffing
rum & nutty pudding

FESTIVE FARE

devils on horseback
stilton pâté
baked ham
gilded gingerbread
chestnut mixture for
profiterole pyramid
whole orange marmalade
mulled wine

WILD WINTER WARMERS

caragheen cream
dulse dollops
sloe gin

TRADITIONAL MENU

chestnut soup
soused herring
roast goose & gooseberry sauce
cloutie dumpling

Stilton, the classic festive cheese, with newcomer, Perthshire Craigrossie. Both cheeses go well with claret and leftover stilton makes an excellent pâté to serve with wine or port

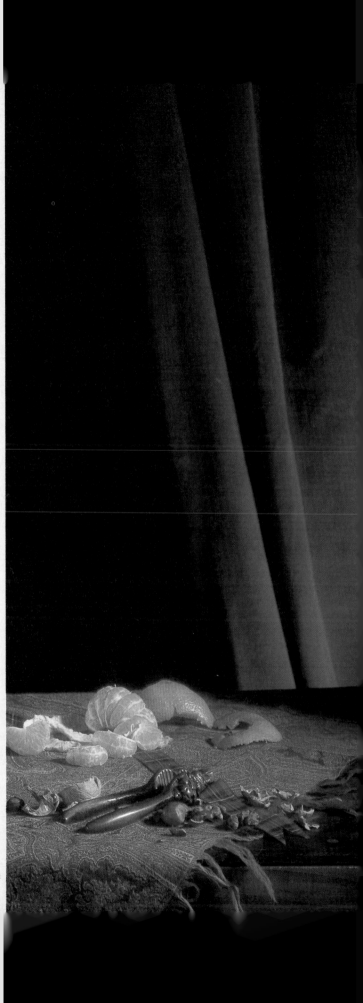

WINTER CHEFS

Neil MacLean

When he was fifteen, **Bill Gibb** worked in his parents' pub - the Lumsden Arms, near Huntly. 'I was put in charge of the steaks on Saturday nights.' Now, at the Craigendarroch Hotel and Country Club in Ballater, Bill's cooking has gone well-beyond steak and chips and, so have customers' tastes and expectations.

Bill Gibb is one of the most innovative of the young Scottish chefs. Building on his early training at Gleneagles and the Station Hotel in Perth, he has developed a highly visual style, winning awards for food that looks as good as it tastes.

Often he will combine two meats or two types of fish on the same plate with a duo of contrasting sauces, and frequently one of the meats will be the local Scottish beef - which he considers to be particularly good in winter.

His butcher, Michael Sheridan, has worked in Ballater for twenty-five years. His shop in the High Street is popular both with locals and visitors and he supplies meat to the Royal Family when they are staying at Balmoral. He buys his beef through the Aberdeen Angus scheme and hangs it in his shop himself. This is the key to top quality beef, and Michael Sheridan believes in hanging it for about three weeks before it is ready.

Bill Gibb is in no doubt that Aberdeen Angus is the best, well hung and with a good marbled texture. He buys a whole side of beef at a time. With the topside he will make his own steak and mushroom pie; with the lower parts, simple dishes, like the Scottish classic - mince, potatoes and skirlie .He likes to marinate prime cuts in a whisky sauce and makes a traditional roast with the sirloin.

With Christmas in mind, Bill will buy a goose from Mill of Botary farm, at Cairnie close to Aberdeen. He might poach this, filled with a mousse of chestnuts and herbs, for a seasonal celebration, to be followed by a dessert to keep winter at bay - a hot drambuie soufflé, perhaps, or bread and butter pudding with a honey sauce.

Peter Jukes has a coal fire at either end of his restaurant to warm his customers. Anstruther, on the East Neuk of Fife can be a cold place to live in winter. Born in Wolverhampton ('cod and chips country,' he says) Peter bought The Cellar Restaurant in 1980 after training at Gleneagles, the Imperial in Torquay, and the Dorchester. His best experience however was cooking at the famous Chewton Glen.

Peter's speciality is fish-cookery and he is well-placed to benefit from the catches of the inshore fishing fleet off the Fife coast. He knows most of the East Neuk fishermen and he often buys his fish before it has landed on the quay - sometimes, in fact, it is too fresh for him to use, so it rests for a day or two before it can be cooked. The rest of his seafood he buys from Keracher's, a long-established family firm in St Andrews.

There cannot be many people living in Scotland who look forward to the onset of winter, but Peter Jukes claims that he does. The fish is better then, he says, as long as the boats have managed to get out to bring it back. Halibut is his favourite fish, and he likes it best when grilled and served without a heavy sauce. He grills it very briefly, for a minute or less, at a very high heat with some citrus juices and a little tarragon. Peter Jukes' style is very simple and straightforward. Everything is cooked at the last minute, each dish in a separate pan. Wine and herbs are his most important ingredients after the fish. It seems that many of the classic fish dishes are on their way back, but the flour has gone and sauces are lighter, and often he will cook fish (like roasted monkfish) on the bone (because, he says, it tastes better) much to the delight of customers who thought that nobody did it that way anymore.

Mussels are very good in winter. Keracher's get them from Inverawe. Peter has his own version of *Mussels Marinières* which has proved very popular. He places the mussels in a large pan with

a touch of *Muscadet*, fish stock, basil, tarragon, chopped onion, leek and carrot. As soon as the mussels start to open he takes them out, finishes off the sauce with a little cream then returns the mussels to the pan, lets them rest for 30 seconds during which time they finish cooking in the steam, and then he rushes them straight to the table.

Further along the coast, at Crail, there is an Irishman called Patrick Reilly who sells fresh crab from a hut beside the harbour. Peter buys these to make his most popular winter dish - haddock *en croute*. He stuffs a haddock fillet with crab, bakes it in puff pastry, then serves it with a shellfish sauce. Sampling that is one very good reason to be in Scotland in winter.

Bill Gibb (above) is one of the best of the innovative young chefs. His highly visual style has won awards for food which looks as good as it tastes
Peter Jukes (right) is well placed to benefit from the catches of the inshore fishing fleet off the Fife coast. He makes fish cooking his speciality

FESTIVITIES AT HOME

Kirsty Burrell

The traditional day for the making of the Christmas pudding was the Sunday before Advent. It brings the first 'frisson' of Christmas excitement. Children in 'pinnies' stand round the kitchen table chopping and stirring; everyone in the house must give the mixture a stir and make a wish. Later, I secretly wrap little silver charms in greaseproof paper and poke them into the heavy brandy-scented mixture. Children do not usually like this kind of rich, fruity pudding very much, but they do like finding the charms. For a more child-oriented festive meal, I make a chocolate ice-cream Yule log, decorated with marzipan holly leaves and berries. We also make Christmas-shaped spicy biscuits, iced and decorated with silver balls to hang on the tree.

Mince pies are excellent things. I make my own mincemeat, but there is no need to - there are some good ones on the market. The secret is to add a dash of brandy just before making the pies. Keep them tiny and they are a quickly-made treat for unexpected visitors. Bake them by the dozen for carol parties and other festive gatherings. I think that at one time dried fruit must have been regarded as the height of luxury in Scotland - perhaps partly a legacy of war-time scarcities. The mixture forms the basis of so many winter treats - mince pies, Christmas pudding, Christmas cake, black bun. I sometimes make a very special gingerbread instead of the traditional rich Christmas cake. I bake it in a big Christmas-tree-shaped tin and decorate it with very thin green-tinted glace icing and gold and silver sugared almonds. This year, however, I intend to try gilding it.

Christmas is the best time for parties. The house is at its prettiest, from the red-beribboned holly wreath on the front door, to the pictures in the hall draped with holly and ivy, decorations made from silver and gold-sprayed cones, nuts and poppy seed-heads, and the drawing-room, pine-scented from the tall dark Christmas tree with its glowing lights and hanging baubles, catching the light of a welcoming log fire in the grate as they turn.

Elizabeth David makes two very important points about preparing food for a party. The first thing is for the hostess not to wear herself out for days beforehand, fussing about with aspic, making patterns with mayonnaise and sticking little things on sticks! You do, after all, want to be in a fit condition to enjoy the party yourself. The second is: 'A very understandable mistake often made at buffet luncheons and suppers is the over-complication of the food and the diversity of the dishes offered. Several fine dishes of attractively prepared food look hospitable and tempting, but it is bewildering to be faced with too many choices, especially if some are hot and some are cold. The taste of the food is lost when you find four or five different things all messed up on your plate at the same time; so have as the most important dish something rather simple which everyone will like, and provide variety with two or three salads.'

A big baked ham, studded with cloves makes an ideal centrepiece for a Christmas party. In the (extremely unlikely) event of there being any left over, cold ham is welcome at hastily assembled suppers in a way that cold turkey is not. Beside the baked ham on its tall white ham stand, I would put my huge soup tureen piled high with baked potatoes, and a bowl of Greek yogurt to put in them. I would add a big kilner jar of spiced plums (which I describe in 'Autumn') and a couple of crisp, colourful salads, full of apples (red and green), celery, nuts and peppers of every hue. Devils on horseback, prunes wrapped in bacon, are fiddly to make but festive and popular.

A spectacular dessert for a Christmas party is an enormous pyramid of profiteroles, filled with a creamy chestnut mixture and doused with dark chocolate sauce. I like to perch a noisy little indoor firework on top and carry it in to a chorus of 'oohs and aahs'!

We always have a baby stilton for the Christmas season, to be presented on a marble slab surrounded by green grapes and oatcakes, and a green glass bowl of those tiny clementines with their glossy leaves still on which come into the shops just before Christmas. Later on in the entertaining season, when the stilton is beginning to look a bit tired, I make stilton pâté to serve with oatcakes or warm cheese sable biscuits (ideal for first-footers).

Mulled wine is a welcome favourite on these occasions. I ladle it from my brass jelly pan, keeping it hot on the Aga. (It must not be allowed to boil). Its spicy aroma welcomes friends as they come through the door, and it warms hands and insides on a cold winter's night. For me, it sums up the 'spirit of Christmas'.

After the long, pleasurable, but hectic, period of celebration and hospitality of Christmas and New Year, I secretly welcome the return to 'auld claes and purrich' towards the end of January. My husband spends evenings leafing through (vegetable) seed catalogues, making ambitious architectural plans for his vegetable plot . . shall we try yellow courgettes, ruby chard or an asparagus bed this year? ('In Highland Perthshire?') Perhaps not; what with the late, wet spring, the rabbits and the early frosts . . . still, in January in Scotland optimism is an important quality.

The cookery year starts for me in the last week of January when the Seville oranges come into the shops, with oranges bobbing in the big brass jelly pan and the rich, tangy smell filling the kitchen. The heaps of glowing fruit cheer me up on grey winter days, reminding me of a February holiday in Andalusia. As a northern European, oranges or lemons actually growing on trees still seems to me an exotic thing. This is the best (and cheapest) time of year for citrus fruits, and there are all sorts of recipes for marmalade - three fruit, grapefruit, with ginger, or even whisky (which I find too strong); but my favourite is the easiest, a simple whole fruit marmalade where the oranges are boiled whole before being chopped, and sugar is added. I add a few lemons to help the set and add tang.

I would not want to make marmalade in June; the seasonal aspect of cooking is one of its joys - new Ayrshire potatoes in June, the first punnets of Carse of Gowrie raspberries at the roadside in July

but it's always worth putting a few Seville oranges in the freezer while they are in season, to add their characteristic flavour to dishes throughout the year. In the past, orange with fish was as popular as lemon is now, and in old cookery books 'an orange' means a bitter, Seville-type orange. I like white fish, such as plaice or turbot, with an orange sauce. Seville orange ice-cream makes a change from the ubiquitous lemon sorbet, and if you add some blood orange juice (I keep some in the freezer too) the colour is beautiful. More mundanely, a favourite winter fruit salad is simply oranges, green grapes and bananas, sliced into a mixture of strained greek yoghurt and honey - children love it.

I try to keep the traditions we have alive; Burns' Night (when you must keep to traditional haggis, tatties and neeps, of course!), St Valentine's Day, Shrove Tuesday, Easter . . . and, perhaps, invent a few more. I met my husband at a party given by a friend to celebrate the first snowdrops in her garden one early February evening - all green and white food and huge paper snowdrops indoors, and candles glowing in jam jars under the still bare apple trees outside.

February is a dreary month in Scotland, and I always make much of St Valentine's Day. The children make heart-shaped biscuits, we cut heart-shaped french toast, and for supper we usually have fish with Seville orange sauce and heart-shaped croutes, followed by a pudding-cake made in a heart-shaped mould. These pudding-cakes are useful to have in one's culinary repertoire and I am always looking for new ones. The chocolate marquise and the cassata (which I describe in 'Summer') are ideal celebration desserts around which to sing 'Happy Birthday'.

WILD WINTER WARMERS

Tess Darwin

During past centuries, as the cold winter weather gradually set in, much effort was put into gathering and storing any wild foods that could be found. They were essential to eke out the precious harvest, which had to last nearly a year in isolated communities with few opportunities to buy in or even barter for anything extra.

One food source that could always be relied upon to provide nourishing winter sustenance was seaweed; some varieties were collected throughout the year but many were dried in spring for winter use. Seaweeds are very nutritious, being particularly high in important minerals such as potassium and magnesium, often lacking in the modern diet. Various kinds were eaten in considerable quantities until quite recently, certainly into the beginning of this century. Martin Martin recorded in *The Western Islands of Scotland* (1716) that four varieties were popular; dulse, linarich, sloke and sea-tangle.

Dulse can be found on rocks around the Scottish coast; it is a purple-red seaweed with flat, fan-like fronds up to a foot long which get broader and tougher with age. It can be bought in health food shops, but whether dried or freshly collected should be thoroughly washed in running water then soaked for a couple of hours. Traditionally this rather leathery seaweed was simmered over a low heat for at least three hours until it became jelly-like, then beaten with butter, salt and pepper, sprinkled with vinegar, and served as a vegetable. Alternatively it was mixed with oatmeal and fried as little patties for breakfast. It can be eaten raw in salads, but many people find it unpalatable, and for modern taste and convenience the best use of dulse is mixed with other vegetables and cooked similarly. Dulse also used to be sun-dried and rolled up to be chewed in place of tobacco, in the days when that was scarce and relatively expensive.

Linarich (Gaelic *linnearach*) was a general name used for Enteromorpha species. These are stringy green seaweeds, like knobbly, elongated

Dulse

runner beans, which are very common on rocky shores. They can be stir-fried in the Chinese manner, or used in soup. **Sloke**, also known as laver or sea-spinach, is a common purple-red seaweed, with irregular, membraneous fronds that turn black and brittle when dry. It was particularly popular in the Western Islands, where it was gathered at the end of winter and after pounding and stewing it with a little water, was eaten with pepper, vinegar, and butter; alternatively it was stewed with leeks and onions. Fried with bacon and rolled in oatmeal, it makes laver-bread.

Several other species were widely eaten, but perhaps the most popular of all to this day is **caragheen** or Irish moss. This seaweed, which is very variable in shape, is red, with flat, much-branched fronds, is found around the coast on all kinds of shore except mud. Again it can be bought in health food shops, but if collected should be taken from low water mark (where there is the least danger of contamination), then thoroughly washed and sun-dried until it turns white, after which it will keep indefinitely. Traditionally it was boiled in milk to make a kind of blancmange, flavoured with jam or lemon juice, known to be a nourishing, strengthening food long before scientific analysis showed that it is rich in vitamins, minerals and iodine.

Silverweed roots, although best eaten fresh in spring (as described earlier), were collected throughout the year and dried for use during winter, ground into flour for porridge or bread. The roots of **spignel** (known in Scots as badminnie, Gaelic *muilceann*) can also be dried and were very popular, adding a spicy flavour similar to lovage in soups and stews. Although nowhere abundant, spignel is fairly common in upland areas of Scotland; it belongs to the cow parsley family, with characteristic heads of tiny, creamy-white flowers, and delicate feathery leaves. Although it is very unlikely that spignel would be confused with anything else, some members of this plant family are poisonous and care should be taken with identification.

Winter was always the time when warming drinks were greatly appreciated, especially in days

Juniper

when the dark, smokey houses were often used only as a shelter from the elements, and most of daily life went on out of doors. A variety of herbs, leaves and berries were dried for winter use as tea.

Thyme was known in Shetland as tae-girse, tea-grass. In Gaelic it was called *lus an rìgh*, the king's plant, because of its reputation for giving courage and strength. Thyme tea is in fact an excellent cough remedy, and generally beneficial for infections of the throat, chest and stomach, making it invaluable in the winter store cupboard of today as much as in earlier times.

Juniper was once more widespread than now, but it can still be found on mountains, moorland and in pine and birch woods scattered throughout Scotland. The small berries, black with a bloom like plums, ripen in their second year on the shrub, and last through the winter making them a useful food supplement. Juniper berries can be dried to make tea or roasted and ground into a kind of coffee, but are best known as the source of the volatile oil used to make gin. Many Highland estates collected wild juniper berries in large quantities for export to the Netherlands until very recently, but now the possibility of commercial production of improved varieties is under investigation.

Sloe, or blackthorn, has berries similar to juniper, and is thought to be a wild ancestor of today's cultivated plum trees. It is a common shrub throughout woods and on roadsides. The fruit should be picked in early winter, after frost has tenderised it, and can be used for wine, but as sloe berries are usually rather sparse they usually need to be combined with other fruits such as hawthorn, elderberry or rosehips. Sloes added to gin make a wonderful pink liqueur, ideal for midwinter cheer.

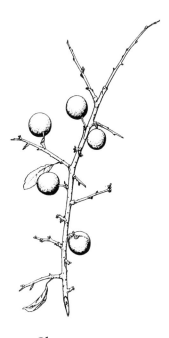

Sloe

Caragheen

TRADITIONAL TABLE

Sandra Macpherson

CHESTNUT SOUP

There is nothing which reminds me of winter evenings more than the aroma of chestnuts cooking on glowing embers, whether on a barrow in a darkened London street or the warm hearth at home. There are not so many sweet chestnut trees in Scotland but they are worth seeking out when the chestnuts begin to fall in late October. They must not be confused, however, with the inedible horse chestnut which produces 'conkers', avidly sought by boys and girls for their games. The sweet chestnut can be eaten raw or cooked, preserved by drying or ground into flour to make sweet porridge - a real old-fashioned treat.

Cooking chestnuts does not require polished culinary skills. There are ways, however, in which they can be well prepared so that they are not undercooked and indigestible or, alternatively, over-cooked, dried out and hard. When roasting chestnuts the secret is to take a sharp knife and make a small slit in each shell except one. The chestnuts are then placed on a shovel in the embers of the fire and left to cook. The moisture inside the unsplit chestnut turns into steam and, consequently, it explodes. This is the signal which indicates that the other chestnuts are now ready for eating. There is an old sixteenth century saying that advises: 'take the chestnuts out of the fire with the cat's paw', and it is wise to remember this as cooked chestnuts are dangerously hot when they come off the cinders.

Chestnuts, cooked on a log fire and served with brandy or liqueurs and coffee make a welcome completion to a winter dinner party. On Christmas day, they might appear in different guises, and if the turkey or goose is not stuffed or served with chestnuts, chestnut soup is an ideal alternative.

SOUSED HERRING

Herring has always been an important food in the Scottish diet and the fish is often referred to as the 'silver darlings'. Wick was the main herring port from the early nineteenth century until the 1930s

and women 'gutters' came from the Isles to gut the fish. They would sit on the sea wall watching for the herring drifters to come in, busily knitting and singing their Gaelic songs. When the drifters went further afield, as far as Yarmouth and Lowestoft, the gutters would follow and remain with them until their work was done. While they worked with the fish they wore cotton bandages on their fingers in case the sharp knives nicked their fingers. The shops in Wick stayed open late on pay day which was Saturday, enabling the women to replenish their knitting wool and purchase other supplies.

After the herring was landed it was put into barrels, salted, and sent as far as the Baltic States and even to Russia. The fish were packed tightly 'like herring in a barrel', as the saying goes, to keep them well preserved. Other fish, like ling and cod, were also preserved in this way and sometimes dried or smoked, producing kippers from herring and 'finnan haddie' from haddock. Fish would be seen drying out on the side of the walls of the houses along the coasts. Soused, or pickled herring is another old method of preserving the fish which is popular today.

ROAST GOOSE

On cold and crisp evenings when light is fading and the sun sinks low in the sky, one may have the good fortune to see a skein of geese flying back from their feeding grounds to roost. Their unfailing sense of direction is fascinating as they fly neatly in formation following behind the leader whose wingbeat makes the air turbulent, easing the flight of the following birds. They use much the same technique on longer autumn migration flights. When the leading bird becomes weary a following bird takes over as the group travel further towards warmth, food and survival.. The sight and the sound of the skeins is one of the consolations of a Scottish winter.

Long before the turkey was introduced to

Britain the delicate soft flavour of goose graced tables at Christmas. More recently, turkey has been widely accepted but the tradition of roast goose is a popular alternative for Christmas dinner once more. People are increasingly keeping geese on their farm or in their back yard and domesticated geese are widely available, though some wild geese are protected at all times and others in the close season (see *Wild Birds and The Law*, RSPB). Wild geese tend to average only 4-6 pounds (2-3 kg) in weight compared with domesticated birds of 20 pounds (10 kg) or more. If such a large bird is not desired, then it is better to ask for a flock gosling, when choosing the domesticated goose.

Goose produces a lot of its own fat and this may be taken off periodically during the cooking time and it is not always necessary to baste the bird. This excess fat is useful for frying other foods later and in former times was often spread over bread for a separate meal. Traditionally goose is served with sage and onion stuffing and apples. Now one often finds recipes with a variety of fruit and nuts in the ingredients. Wild rice, apricots and dates make an interesting combination of flavours for a stuffing and gooseberry sauce adds a clean sharp taste to the meat.

CLOUTIE DUMPLING

Cloutie dumpling is one of the oldest puddings and still very popular. In the days of open fire cooking and no ovens, many of the puddings were steamed in the big black pot. Cloutie dumpling is made in a cloth, 'clout' in Scots. In the north it was also called a 'duff', and many from the far north will tell you that the cloutie dumpling was very much a part of their staple diet. Any leftovers on the day it was cooked were fried the following day for breakfast or for the midday meal and were equally as delicious.

This pudding was traditionally the Christmas pudding in Scotland. One would find the usual surprises in the cloutie dumpling as in the richer Christmas pudding: a silver coin for wealth, a button for a bachelor, a thimble for an old maid and a horseshoe for luck. Custard was often poured over the cloutie dumpling, though nowadays cream or a sauce may be preferred.

CLARET

There is continuity as well as comfort in the warming winter wines and spirits of Scotland. Today you can still browse among the bottles of the wine merchant, Cockburn & Co., who supplied Sir Walter Scott with his 1815 *Chateau Lafite*, you can sample one of Scotland's finest cellars at Houstoun House, once home of Shairp of Houstoun, a leading eighteenth century wine merchant; and you can enjoy a glass of claret in the Vintner's Room of The Vaults in Leith, where the whole great and glorious tradition of importing Bordeaux wines began as early as the twelfth century. And, if your purse can bear it, you can even follow the example of Glasgow City Council, which in 1714 ordered, on behalf of a local MP, Daniel Campbell of Shawfield, no less than two hogsheads of *Chateau Haut Brion* - enough wine to fill 536 bottles.

'Les Anglais viennent peu a Bordeaux; on y voit quelques Ecossais,' noted a French official in 1699. And over the following decades this trend became ever more apparent. While the English turned increasingly to port, Scotland remained loyal to claret. It became Scotland's 'other national drink' (beer being the staple) enjoyed alike - as Billy Kay and Cailean Maclean relate in their fine book, *Knee Deep in Claret* - by the grandest in the land and humble fishermen in loch-side howffs.

The stern, strong qualities of good Bordeaux wine were seen as the very embodiment of national character. Poor Tobias Smollett, homesick in London, despaired of a city wallowing in flabby roast beef and flaccid port while:

Firm and erect the Caledonian stood

Old was his mutton and his claret good.

The author of this doggerel was that proto-McGonagall, John Home. His patriotism extended to goading his philosopher namesake for anglicising the spelling of his surname. But David Hume had the last laugh. In his will he left John several cases of port, on condition that his tormentor sign for them as John Hume!

Generic claret was the drink of the age, but towards the end of the eighteenth century imports became subject to heavier duties and Scots increasingly adopted the approach recommended by every modern wine merchant: if tax is on quantity, go for quality. Wine still arrived at Leith in hogsheads rather than bottles, but the orders placed with such Bordeaux negociants as the Ulster-Scots house of Johnston were now more often for vintage wine from the Chateaux of *Lafite, Latour, Leoville, Kirwan, Bergeron, Cauvale, Duluc, Margaux, Mouton, Rauzan* and *Haut Brion.*

NEW FOOD, NEW WINE

So you can still enjoy claret from the same vineyards and merchants which supplied Enlightenment Scotland. But Daniel Campbell's *Haut Brion*, which cost him £70, would set the present day drinker back close on £20 000. If you want to find wines which share the qualities of good claret and don't break the bank, which come from vintners who take the same delight in innovation as the new breed of Scottish chefs, and which maintain the Scottish connection, you could do no better than turn to Australia. For if Scots played their role as merchants, negociants and, above all, consumers of the wines of Bordeaux, in Australia they were the very founding fathers of the wine industry.

The first notable figure in Australian vinicultural history, John Macarthur, who came of an Argyll family, landed at Sydney in 1790, just two years after the arrival of the First Fleet. He was a colourful character, remembered for dubious business deals which brought him huge estates, the introduction of the Merino sheep and his constant quarrels with successive colonial governors, most notably the much-maligned William Bligh, of Bounty fame. As a result of his feud with Bligh, Macarthur found in Europe in 1815 and took the opportunity to tour the vineyards of France. On his return to Australia he planted the first Antipodean vineyard at Camden, just south of Sydney.

The man who is generally recognised as the Father of Australian Wine, however, was James Busby, born and brought up in Edinburgh, who arrived in the colony aged twenty-three, in 1824, where he took up a holding of 2000 acres in the Hunter Valley. Busby already had an interest in wine and he published his *Treatise on the Culture of the Vine and the Art of Making Wine* in Sydney, just a year after his arrival.

A visit to France and Spain in 1831 led to two further publications and, more importantly, the collection of no less than 678 vine cuttings. These formed the basis of the vine stock in the Hunter Valley and, even today, every glass of wine from this now major vinicultural centre is likely to have come from offshoots of vines collected by the pioneering Scotsman.

Busby may have written the first book on wine to be published in Australia, but the first treatise specifically concerned with the wine of the new Continent, was the work of another Scot, Dr Alexander Kelly, whose *Winegrowing in Australia* appeared in 1861. Kelly was also an early South Australian vintner. His vineyards at Trinity and McLaren Vale, both near Adelaide, were not, however, a commercial success. In the 1870s McLaren Vale was sold to Thomas Hardy, whose name is still to be found on some of Australia's best-known wines.

Kelly was one of a number of doctors who pioneered Australian wine growing; another was Dr Penfold, the man who gave his name to most famous wine to come out of the country, Penfold's Grange Hermitage, the 1978 vintage of which finally convinced Europe that Australia could produce world-class wines.

Finally, there were the Scotsmen who pioneered wine growing in the developing areas around the coast of Australia. Another doctor, John Ferguson, established the first western Australian vineyard, on the Swan River, in 1859. John Riddoch settled

Coonawara, in eastern South Australia in the 1860s and, in 1890, encouraged by a fellow Scot, a gardener named William Wilson, planted the first vines in an area which has since become one of the most reknowned wine producing areas of Australia.

PORT

There is an obvious question mark which hangs over any discussion of port. If the drink was so scorned by Scots, how do we account for the host of Scottish names which we associate with port: Cockburn, Dow, Graham, Sandeman? The answer lies in a good, old-fashioned Scots triumph of commercialism over patriotism.

With the imposition of heavier duties on French imports, Scots finally turned to port and Scottish merchants soon found their way to Portugal. George Sandeman of Perth, described in 1809, as 'Mr Sandeman, the head of a great Wine House in Oporto', was one of the first. Graham's was originally a Glasgow company trading in such general items as cloth and cotton which established a Portuguese branch in 1820. They acquired a bad debt which could only be recovered in the form of port. The irritation of the parent company at this turned to pleasure when the port was snapped up by Scottish customers - and a great Port House was born. Robert Cockburn, younger brother of Henry, Lord Cockburn, the great Scottish Lawyer, went to Portugal in 1814. His name was to become associated with no less than two substantial wine merchants - of which Cockburn & Co. (Leith) still thrives - and a famous port company.

MALT WHISKY

Scotland's own supreme contribution to winter warmth was a relatively late developer. While eighteenth century Scotland refined its taste for claret, malt whisky, the grain-based product of lowland distilleries was, in Burn's words, 'a most rascally liquor', and the distillation of the real thing, Highland malt whisky, remained a largely illicit, cottage industry.

Only as late as the 1820s did two events lay the foundations of the modern whisky industry: the

1823 Excise Act encouraged legal distilling and the invention of the patent still encouraged large-scale production of the quality of grain spirit which provided the base for blended whiskies. George Smith of Upper Drumin in Glenlivet, a well-educated farmer who had trained as an architect, was one of the first to take advantage of 1823. He discarded his illicit still - one of over 200 in Glenlivet alone at the time - and built the original Smith's Glenlivet distillery.

Glenlivet soon became a centre of malt whisky production, as did Islay and Campbelltown, though notable distilleries were to be found everywhere in Scotland from Rosebank, outside Falkirk, to Highland Park on Orkney. This geographical spread has contributed to a very real variety in taste which makes malt whisky so remarkable among world-class spirits.

Until relatively recently, however, almost all malt production was blended into famous brand name whiskies. This has made individual distilleries somewhat vulnerable to fluctuations in demand and over twenty of them have closed down during the past decade alone. Malt whisky fans complain that some of these losses are the equivalent of losing a *Lafite* or *Pétrus*. Over the past twenty years, of course, things have changed. The pure malt production of almost every distillery is now freely available - and there is no reason why demand for them should not subsist quite happily alongside that for the popular blends. After all, whoever heard of demand for *Grand Crus* undermining demand for good generic *Graves?*

RECIPES

CULLEN SKINK

For this you should use pale finnan haddock, called after the village of Finnan, near Aberdeen, not orange-dyed fish.

1 large finnan haddock
1oz(25g) butter
1 small onion
1 pint(600ml) milk
mashed potato to thicken
chives or parsley to garnish

Pour milk over the fish, bring just to the boil, cover and leave for half an hour to steep. Meanwhile soften the onion in the butter. Drain the haddock, reserving the liquid, and skin and flake the flesh from the bone. Liquidise the onion with a little of the milk in which the haddock was cooked and sufficient mashed potato to thicken.. Mix in the flaked fish and the rest of the cooking liquid and serve garnished with chopped chives or parsley. This soup is excellent chilled, with the addition of a small carton of yogurt. (Kirsty Burrell)

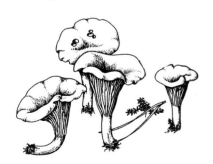

CHESTNUT SOUP

1¼lb(550g) chestnuts
1 pint(600ml) milk
1½oz(40g) butter
1 teaspoon sugar
1 pint(600ml) white stock
salt and ground black pepper
1 tablespoon brandy
10fl oz(300ml) double cream

Shell the chestnuts and put them into boiling water for about 5 minutes. Scrape, and wash them in cold water and put in a pan with 10floz(300ml) milk and enough water to cover. Bring to the boil and allow to simmer until tender. Save 4-6 whole chestnuts putting the rest through a sieve or make a puree in a food processor. Melt butter in a pan, stir in the sugar and chestnut puree. Gradually add stock and remaining milk. Bring to boil then stir in brandy and almost half of the cream. Season with freshly ground black pepper and salt. Whip remaining cream and chop the whole chestnuts. Serve soup hot with a little whipped cream topped with chopped chestnuts.
(Sandra Macpherson)

CHANTERELLE OR WILD MUSHROOM SOUP

1lb(450g) chanterelles or wild mushrooms
1 small onion
4oz(100g) butter
1 pint(600ml) white stock
salt and freshly ground pepper
1oz(25g) flour
10fl oz(300ml) milk
5fl oz(150ml) double cream
few sprigs rosemary

Clean chanterelles or wild mushrooms thoroughly, discard the end of the stalk and roughly chop the remainder. Chop the onion and place in a pan with half of the butter and fry until transparent. Add chanterelles or mushrooms and continue to fry for a few minutes. Add stock, season well and simmer gently for about an hour. Allow to cool. Melt remaining butter in a small pan and stir in the flour. Place this and the other cooked ingredients into a food processor with the milk and process until smooth. Pour soup back into a large pan and cook gently for a few minutes. Serve with a little cream and a sprig of rosemary on top of each bowl of soup.
(Sandra Macpherson)

PARTAN BREE

1 large crab
3oz(75g) rice
1 pint(600ml) milk
1 pint(600ml) white stock
5fl oz(150ml) cream
a little brandy (optional)

If the crab is alive, boil it in salted water for 10 to 15 minutes then remove from the pan and allow to cool. Remove the claws and legs from the cooked crab then crack the claws and remove flesh. Discard any bony cartilage. If you want to take the meat out of the legs break each one at the joints and pick it out with a skewer. Prise the body of the crab open and take out all the edible meat, discarding the gills and stomach sac.

Boil the rice in the milk until tender. Keep the meat from the claws aside. Place the rest of the crab meat, stock, rice and milk into a blender. Season to taste. Pour soup into a pot and bring to the boil. Remove from heat, stir in the cream and add the meat from the claws. Just before serving add a dash of brandy. Garnish each soup bowl with mustard cress.
(Sandra Macpherson)

CLEAR HARE SOUP AND QUENELLES

1 hare
2 carrots
1 large onion
1 small turnip
4 stalks celery
3 pints(1.7 litres) beef stock
1 sprig of rosemary and thyme
½ teaspoon cloves
1 teaspoon black peppercorns
1 blade of mace
2 egg whites and shells
dry sherry (optional)

Skin and joint the hare or ask a butcher to do this. Chop all vegetables and put them in a large saucepan with the hare and stock. Add herbs and spices. Bring to boil then boil for one hour or until hare is well cooked. Lift out the hare and remove 8oz. of the best pieces of the meat keeping this aside for the quenelles. Put the remaining meat and bones back into the stock and simmer for another half hour. Strain through a fine sieve and allow to cool. When cold remove any fat off the top with a spoon and pour soup back into a saucepan. Add whisked egg whites and shells. Bring to boil then simmer until the soup looks clear. Strain twice, season to taste and serve with a little sherry and quenelles.
Quenelles:
8oz(225g) cooked hare
½oz(15g) butter
1oz(25g) flour
2fl oz(50ml) water
1 egg
salt, pepper

Melt butter in a pan gradually adding the flour and water. Cook until it forms a thick paste, then set it aside to cool. Mince or blend the hare and put through a fine sieve. Pound this together with the paste and egg. Season with salt and pepper. To shape the quenelles, dip a teaspoon in hot water, fill it with the mixture and smooth it into an oval shape with a knife (which has also been dipped in hot water). Place the quenelles in a buttered saucepan and pour in sufficient water to half-cover them. Cover with greased paper and poach until they are firm, turning when they are half-cooked. This will take about 15 minutes.
(Sandra Macpherson)

CREAM OF COURGETTE AND ROSEMARY SOUP

2lb(900kg) courgettes
8oz(225g) onions
¾ dessertspoon dried rosemary
2oz(50g) butter
chicken stock

Sauté onions in butter until soft. Add courgettes, rosemary and a little stock and simmer until soft. Liquidise and pass through a sieve. Reheat, adding more stock if necessary, but retain thick consistency, and season. Serve with a swirl of cream and croutons.
(Betty Allen)

TURNIP AND PINE KERNEL SOUP

1 onion chopped
2lb(900g) turnip
2oz(50g) butter
3 pints(1.7 litres) chicken stock
½ cup pine kernels

Sweat the onion and turnip in the butter in a covered pan for a few minutes. Add the chicken stock. Cook for 1 hour then liquidise. Lightly brown the pine kernels in a very lightly buttered pan. Add to soup and keep warm.
(Peter Jukes)

WATERCRESS AND POTATO POTAGE

A creamy soup in which the peppery flavour of watercress is well balanced with the potatoes.

8oz(200g) watercress
2oz(50g) butter
2 large potatoes
10fl oz(300ml) stock
10fl oz(300ml) milk
black pepper

Dice the potatoes, and sauté them gently in the butter, stirring frequently, until they are turning golden. Wash the watercress thoroughly and drain well. Retain a few leaves for garnish; toss the rest with the potatoes for a few minutes. Add the stock and simmer until the potatoes are cooked. Liquidise, then add the milk and pepper and reheat. Garnish with watercress leaves before serving.
(Tess Darwin)

NETTLE BROTH

8oz(200g) young nettle tops
(best April to June)
1 medium onion
2oz(50g) butter
1oz(25g) flour
1oz(25g) oatmeal
1 pint(600ml) milk
seasoning

Wash nettles and remove tougher stems. Boil gently in minimal water with lid on pan for 15 minutes. Drain and mash or liquidise nettles. Melt butter in pan and saute onion until transparent. Stir in flour and oatmeal, cook gently for 2 minutes. Gradually add milk over low heat, then nettles. Season. Simmer for 5 minutes then serve.
(Tess Darwin)

STILTON PATE

An ideal way to use up the tired end of a Christmas stilton.

8oz(225g) ricotta or curd cheese
2 tablespoons dry white wine
a little milk
6oz(175g) stilton
salt, pepper, nutmeg

Grate the stilton. Beat together the ricotta and white wine, add the stilton, and enough milk to give a smooth paste. Season to taste with salt, pepper and nutmeg. Wrap in foil, rolling it to a cylindrical shape. Chill in the fridge for at least an hour. Serve with oatcakes and slices of pear or green apple and walnuts.
(Kirsty Burrell)

CROWDIE EGGS

4 - 6 eggs
3 pints(1.7 litres) milk
1 teaspoon rennet
salt
1 clove crushed garlic
1 tablespoon double cream
chives
parsley
oatcakes
4 - 6 quails eggs (optional)

Hard boil the eggs and allow to cool. If you have quails eggs leave them in their shell after cooking. Warm the milk to blood heat, stir in the rennet and leave to set. This takes about an hour. Once the curd has formed cut it up and leave in a warm place for about 45 minutes, until the whey rises to the top. Turn this into a colander and allow to drain. When all the whey has drained out put the curds into a bowl and mix the garlic into it. Season to taste and stir in the cream.
Shell the hens eggs cut in half and take out the yolks. Place some of the crowdie into each half egg and arrange them in a circle on a large plate. Chop the yolks and the chives, and sprinkle them on top of the filled eggs. Fill the centre of the plate with any extra crowdie and garnish with fresh parsley and quails eggs. Serve with homemade oatcakes.
(Sandra Macpherson)

KIPPER PATE

Kippers, being very strongly flavoured, make the best of the smoked fish pâtés or pastes, easily made in the liquidiser or food processor.

1 kipper (preferably undyed)
an equal weight of unsalted butter
salt, cayenne pepper and lemon
juice to taste

Pour boiling water over the kipper and leave for 5 mins. Drain and remove skin and bones. Put butter cut in pieces and kipper in liquidiser and process till smooth. Season to taste. If the pâté is not being served immediately cover, when cool and set, with clarified butter and foil. It should keep like this for a week or two. This recipe also works for finnan haddock or smokies. For smoked salmon, mackerel, trout or smoked cods' roe omit the steeping in boiling water. Cream cheese can be substituted for half the butter, but this mixture doesn't keep so well.
(Kirsty Burrell)

GOAT'S CHEESE IN FILO PASTRY WITH BASIL AND PINENUTS

Serves 4
2 cloves of garlic
large bunch of fresh basil
3oz(75g) pinenuts toasted
3 tablespoons extra virgin olive oil
3 tablespoons grated hard cheese
8 round slices of goat's cheese
½"(1cm) thick
3 sheets of filo pastry
melted butter

Pound sliced garlic and a little salt with a pestle and mortar. Grind 2oz(50g) of the pinenuts and incorporate along with shredded basil. Pour in the olive oil and work until smooth. Stir in 2oz(50g) of the cheese. Prepare the filo by putting melted butter between the layers, then divide into four. Put 1 teaspoon of the basil mixture on each, followed by one slice of cheese, then more basil mixture and another layer of cheese to form a sort of sandwich. Carefully wrap the cheese sandwich in the filo to make a parcel, binding the edges with more melted butter. Turn over and sprinkle the top with the remaining cheese and pinenuts and place on a baking sheet. Cook in a hot oven 400°F (200°C, mark 6) for 12-15 minutes. Serve with a little home grown salad.
(Alison Parsons)

MUSHROOMS STUFFED WITH HAGGIS

Medium sized button mushrooms stuffed with haggis. Dipped in egg and then ruskoline. Deep fry and serve on a bed of lettuce with a wedge of lemon. Allow 3 to 5 per person depending on size. Variations: stuff with cream cheese or pâté.
(Peter Jukes)

DEVILS ON HORSEBACK

A delicious, festive titbit to serve with drinks, easily made with stoned, or pitted prunes from a wholefood shop, which do not need to be soaked.

Equal quantities of:
prunes
blanched whole almonds (salted if you like)
thinly cut smoked streaky bacon rashers

Fill the cavity of each prune with an almond. Wrap the prunes in pieces of bacon, fasten with a cocktail stick and lay them in a foil-lined baking tray and grill until the bacon is crispy.
(Kirsty Burrell)

MOUSSELINE OF SCALLOPS WITH CHAMPAGNE AND CHIVE SAUCE

For the mousseline:
12oz(350g) scallops, coral removed
8oz(225g) sole, skin removed
18fl oz(500ml) double cream
salt and cayenne pepper
For the sauce:
¾ pint(425ml) champagne
¾ pint(425ml) chicken stock
1 shallot

Mince scallops and sole in food processor. Keeping cool in a bowl of ice, put everything through a sieve and leave in fridge until required. Preheat oven to 375°F (190°C, mark 5). Gradually beat in cream using an electric hand whisk, season to taste. Put into lightly buttered ramekins and tap gently to get rid of air. Cook in bain marie for 25 minutes until just firm. Remove from water and leave for 5 minutes before turning out.

Sauce:

Reduce champagne, stock and shallot until it is syrupy - about 2 tablespoons. Add cream and reduce to required consistency, sieve, reheat and season. Add finely chopped chives just before serving. Pour some on plate and set mousseline on top, garnish with a little lumpfish roe.
(Betty Allen)

CHILLED ROULADE OF SMOKED SALMON AND SOLE MOUSSE

Serves 8
thin slices of best quality smoked Tay salmon
8oz(225g) lemon sole fillets
15fl oz(425ml) double cream
1 egg white
1 teaspoon finely chopped parsley
1 teaspoon finely chopped chervil
1 teaspoon finely chopped chives
nutmeg
5fl oz(150ml) natural yogurt
1 tablespoon sherry vinegar
½ cucumber

Cover a piece of tin foil 12"x8"(30x20cm) with the thin slices of smoked salmon.
Liquidise the lemon sole fillets with the egg white, a good pinch of salt and 5fl oz(150ml) double cream. Pass this through a fine sieve, then place in a bowl and set over ice to chill for 5 minutes. Carefully beat in most of the remaining cream mixing thoroughly between each addition. At this point, test a little of the mousseline by poaching a teaspoonful in hot water. Adjust consistency with more cream if the mouseline feels too firm, then season with salt, pepper, nutmeg and fold in the herbs. Spread an even layer of the mousseline over the smoked salmon, then carefully roll up like a Swiss roll, twist the ends of the foil to seal. Place in a large pot or fish kettle, cover with boiling water, then poach very slowly for 30 minutes, remove and allow to cool, then chill in the fridge.
Prepare the dressing by cutting half the cucumber into matchstick pieces allow to drain for 10 minutes, then dry on a kitchen towel. Mix the natural yogurt with the sherry vinegar, then add to the cucumber. With a sharp knife, cut through the foil into ½"(1cm) slices, remove the foil then arrange on a plate and serve with the cucumber dressing.
(Bruce Sangster)

98

MUSSELS WHISKY CREAM

1lb(450g) mussels (cooked and shelled)
2 slices white bread
4oz(100g) butter
1 small onion
1 clove garlic
¼ green pepper
¼ red pepper
1½oz(40g) flour
5fl oz(150ml) buttermilk
5fl oz(150ml) cream
2 tablespoons whisky
freshly ground pepper and salt

Make breadcrumbs with the white bread, fry in half of the butter and set aside. Chop onion, garlic and peppers finely and fry in the remaining butter until cooked. Stir the flour into pan and gradually pour in the buttermilk making a thick sauce. Season with black pepper and salt. Place mussels into sauce and cook for a further few minutes. Stir in the whisky and cream and pour into a deep serving dish. Sprinkle fried breadcrumbs on top and serve immediately with brown bread.
(Sandra Macpherson)

SOUSED HERRING

4-6 filleted herrings
2 bay leaves
4 cloves
12 peppercorns
1 dessertspoon chopped parsley
1 blade mace
1 small onion
2oz(50g) butter
salt and pepper
15fl oz(425ml) wine vinegar

Season herrings with pepper and salt, keeping skin to the outside. Soften the butter and mix the parsley into it. Spread the parsley butter over the flesh of the herrings and roll up each one from head to tail. Place in an ovenproof dish. Slice onion finely and place on top of the fish along with all other herbs and spices. Mix the vinegar with an equal amount of water or enough to almost cover the fish. Cover and place in a preheated oven at 250°F (130°C, mark 2) for one hour. Allow fish to cool in its liquid. Remove fish from dish and serve cold with brown bread and butter.
(Sandra Macpherson)

GLAZED LOCH LINNHE PRAWNS WITH GARLIC AND HERB BUTTER

6 Dublin Bay prawns or langoustines
per person
8oz(225g) unsalted butter
small bunches of tarragon, parsley, chervil, chives finely chopped and mixed together
2 egg yolks
1 bulb chopped garlic
salt and pepper
juice of half a lemon

Blanch the washed live prawns in boiled water for 1 minute and refresh them in ice water (blanching them makes peeling the shell off much easier). Separate the tails from the head, peel the tails and run a knife down the middle to remove the intestine.
Meanwhile, using a food mixer whip the butter, egg yolks and herbs and crushed garlic until it becomes light in texture and white in colour. Also add a little seasoning and juice of half a lemon.
To serve: reheat the blanched prawn tails in hot water or a steamer, when hot fold them into the whipped soft butter and place into a deep soup style dish. Place the dish under the grill until golden brown and garnish with a hot prawn head.
(Graham Newbould)

MARINATED TROUT

1 large trout
caster sugar
coarse salt
crushed black peppercorns
crushed white peppercorns
bunch of dill

Gut the trout. Remove head and tail. Then remove the bones. To do this cut along one side of the backbone and expose the ribs. Keeping the knife against the bones gradually pare away the upper fillet. Then hold the backbone with one hand and pare away the lower fillet. For every 1lb(450g) of fish mix together 2 tablespoons of sugar, 2 tablespoons coarse salt and one spoonful of mixed black and white peppercorns. Place the fish skin downward and gently rub this mixture into the flesh, even quantities on both fillets. Place a sprig of dill between the fillets and close them together with the skin outside. Wrap tightly in aluminium foil and place in fridge with a weight on top. Turn twice each day. Prepare this dish at least two days before required. To serve: drain the fish, remove dill and peppercorns then slice thinly. Serve with brown bread and butter and wedges of lemon.
(Sandra Macpherson)

TWEED KETTLE (*BAKED FILLET OF SALMON WITH MUSHROOMS*)

Serves 4
4 fillets of fresh salmon (about 6oz(175g) each)
2 chopped shallots
8oz(225g) mushrooms
5fl oz(150ml) Muscat de Beaumes de Venise (or other sweet wine)
½ pint(300ml) light chicken stock
a little grated nutmeg
2 hard-boiled eggs - whites chopped, yolks sieved
handful of chopped chives
beurre manie (if required)

Place salmon fillets in an oven dish on a bed of chopped shallots. Add salt and pepper and cover with stock and wine. Cover with buttered paper and cook in a hot oven 400°F (200°C, mark 6) for 10 minutes. Meanwhile quarter the mushrooms and cook gently in butter. When the salmon is cooked, add the salmon juices and shallots to the mushrooms. Bring to the boil and reduce a little. Add nutmeg and taste for seasoning. Add *beurre manie* if required to thicken slightly, then stir in 1oz(25g) cold diced butter and chopped chives. Serve salmon with sauce poured over, and top with chopped egg white and sieved yolk and more chives.
(Alison Parsons)

PARCELS OF WILD SALMON AND TURBOT

Serves 4
4 x 2oz(50g) pieces of salmon fillet free of skin and bone
4 x 2oz(50g) pieces of turbot fillet free of skin and bone
1oz(25g) finely chopped shallots
1oz(25g) chopped dill
4oz(100g) finely chopped wild mushrooms (preferably chanterelles picked in Perthshire)
4 large cabbage leaves, preferably spring greens
20 tails of langoustine, de-veined, blanched and shelled
6 tomatoes blanched, skinned and de-seeded
10fl oz(300ml) fish stock
5fl oz(150ml) noilly prat
10fl oz(300ml) double cream
4oz(100g) butter
1oz(25g) caviar

Prepare a *duxelle* by sweating the shallots in 1oz(25g) of the butter, add the wild mushrooms and cook for 2 minutes. To this add 3 tablespoons of the double cream, bring to the boil, add the dill, season then remove and allow to go cold.
Butter four 6"(15cm) square pieces of foil. Blanch and refresh the cabbage leaves, drain and dry on a kitchen cloth. Lay out the cabbage leaves, place a piece of salmon on each, crown with a spoonful of the cold *duxelle*, top with the turbot, then wrap with the cabbage. Place on the foil and seal them tightly. Place in a small pot steamer and gently steam over boiling water for 12 minutes. Meanwhile, reduce the fish stock

by half by boiling. To this add the Noilly Prat and reduce again, add the remaining double cream and reduce to a light coating consistency, season with salt, pepper and lemon juice. To this add ½oz(15g) caviar and 1oz(25g) cold butter. Store hot but do not boil again.

Cut the tomatoes in ¼"(½cm) dice and quickly sauté. Sauté the langoustine tails.

To serve arrange 5 teaspoons of the tomato around the 4 serving plates, crown with the langoustine tails, then remove the parcels from the steamer, unwrap them and cut almost completely in half. Place in the centre of each plate so as to display the centre of the parcels, divide the remaining caviar by placing a little in the centre of the parcels and finish by bordering with the caviar sauce.
(Bruce Sangster)

OYSTERS WITH WHITE WINE

18 oysters (6 or 9 per person)
2 tablespoons of melted butter
cayenne pepper
1 glass dry white wine
(Muscadet, Chablis etc)
salt

Melt the butter, add the oysters (retain oyster juice). Cook them a minute or two. Add wine and oyster juice. Make all thoroughly hot and add a pinch or two of cayenne and a pinch of salt. Serve on hot buttered toast which will absorb the liquid. (John Noble)

FRESH OYSTERS

The dedicated oyster purist would insist on eating oysters freshly opened in the deep side of the shell.

If you can fill a large, deep soup plate with crushed ice it makes a good bed for six open oysters. Then place a strand or two of seaweed around the oysters to give an extra zest of the sea. Black ground pepper, a wedge of lemon and brown bread and butter are suggested accompaniments.

A short cut to opening oysters, if you have no knife, is to pop them in the deep freeze for an hour or so. The frost opens the oysters. Simply cut the muscle attaching the meat to the two sides of the shell but take the greatest care to retain all the natural juice in the deep sides of the shell. A knife is preferred. (John Noble)

OYSTERS GRILLED WITH CHEESE

An easy to prepare oyster dish particularly suitable for those who do not think they like fresh oysters. Open the oysters (large if possible) detach from the shell and put a dessertspoon of thick cream in each shell alongside some of the oyster's own juice. Dust very lightly with parmesan cheese. Sprinkle with melted butter and a tablespoon of dry white wine. Grill under a hot grill for 3-4 minutes. (John Noble)

OYSTERS AND BACON

6-9 oysters per head
1 rasher lightly pre-grilled bacon per head

This favourite Edwardian savoury makes an excellent starter: using one skewer per person open oysters, detach from shells, skewer with a square of bacon between each oyster and grill for 3-4 minutes. Be careful not to overcook. Serve with lemon and a dash of red pepper.
(John Noble)

SQUAT LOBSTER RAVIOLIS WITH A SEA URCHIN SAUCE

Serves 4
For the ravioli paste:
8oz(225g) flour
1¼fl oz(30ml) oil
3¾fl oz(90ml) water
salt
16 squat lobster or Dublin Bay prawns
3 sea urchins
1 pint(600ml) fish stock
4fl oz(100ml) double cream or 3fl oz(75ml) creme fraiche
a little picked chervil
grated fresh ginger
seasoning
2oz(50g) butter

Take the flour, oil, water and two large pinches of salt and mix into a smooth paste. Allow to rest for 24 hours on a tray with a little vegetable oil covered in cling film. Peel the squat lobster. Cut sea urchins in half, remove and keep the roe.

Roll the paste out very thin, place a lobster at ½"(1cm) intervals only on half of it. Season with salt, pepper and a little ginger. Brush the other half with a little water and fold over the lobsters. Use a cutter slightly bigger than the fish and cut out the raviolis, dust with a little flour and let them rest.

Reduce the fish stock by half, add the roes and the cream, reduce, strain through a sieve. Check the seasoning and keep warm. Bring a fairly large pan to the boil with plenty of salt. Throw in the raviolis and simmer for 3-4 minutes, drain and keep warm. Bring the sauce back to the boil, add the chervil and stir the butter into the sauce till it disappears. Divide the raviolis between four plates and coat with the sauce.
(Peter Jackson)

FILLET OF LEMON SOLE WITH CHIVE AND SCAMPI MOUSSE RESTING ON A CRAYFISH SAUCE WITH TENDER YOUNG LEEKS

Serves 4
4 live crayfish
4 fillets of lemon sole
For the scampi mousse:
6oz(168g) shelled scampi (use head and shells for crayfish sauce)
lemon sole
1 egg white
10fl oz(300ml) double cream
½oz(14g) finely snipped chives
For the crayfish caviar sauce:
1 pint(600ml) crayfish stock
4oz(112g) diced carrot, onion and celery
1 pint(600ml) fish stock
1 clove garlic
2 sprigs tarragon
2oz(56g) tomato paste
1oz(28g) oil
seasoning
10fl oz(300ml) double cream
1oz(28g) caviar or salmon eggs (Keta)
1oz(28g) butter
4oz(112g) young tender leeks (leeks should be no thicker than ½"(1cm) thick)

Lightly flatten lemon sole fillets. Shell scampi and remove spinal cord. Cut scampi and sole into small pieces. Place in blender along with egg white and blend until smooth (2-3 minutes). Place into bowl set over ice. Slowly add the double cream and chives. Spread mousse evenly over lemon sole fillets.

Roll up and wrap with cling film. Place in pan with a litle white wine and fish stock (made from the bones). Poach under a lid for 5 minutes until fish is firm. Do not boil. Remove cling film and keep warm.

Heat oil in solid based pan. Sweat down bones of scampi with diced vegetables, garlic, tomato paste and tarragon for 10 minutes, add brandy and fish stock. Simmer for 45 minutes. Pass through a strainer into clean pan, reduce by half, add cream, reduce to coating consistency, pass through fine strainer, bring to boil, finish with hard butter and caviar, mix thoroughly.

Cut leek into 1½"(4cm) long at a slight angle, cook in a little boiling salted water for 3 minutes and keep warm.

Cook crayfish in boiling salted water for 2 minutes. Keep warm. Remove fish from cooking stock and cut two slices from each fillet at a slight angle. Place the remaining piece of sole on plate arranging slices around it. Finish with sauce and decorate with a small bundle of leeks and whole crayfish.
(Bill Gibb)

FAT HEN FLAN

8oz(200g) fat hen leaves
(best June to October)
8oz(200g) shortcrust pastry
3 medium spring onions or
2 tablespoons fresh chives
3 medium eggs
10fl oz(300ml) milk
seasoning, including ground
nutmeg

Wash leaves and remove stems. Boil in minimal water for 15-20 minutes until tender. Drain very well then mash and leave to cool. Line 8"(20cm) flan dish with pastry and add leaves and finely chopped spring onions or chives. Beat eggs and milk with seasoning and pour over leaves. Sprinkle generously with nutmeg. Bake at 375°F (190°C, mark 5) for 30-40 minutes until set and golden brown. Serve hot or cold.
(Tess Darwin)

SUPPER EGGS

A simple supper dish that can be made from the contents of the larder. Quantities are flexible.

4 tablespoons olive oil
1 Spanish onion
2 cloves garlic
salt & pepper
2oz(50g) smoked streaky bacon
1 small chorizo or other spicey cooking sausage
1 pepper (red or green)
2 potatoes, peeled and cubed
1 tin tomatoes
1 small packet of frozen peas
6 eggs

Par boil the potatoes. Put olive oil in a heavy based pan on low heat. Chop the onion and soften in oil. Add garlic crushed with salt and pepper. Stir in chopped streaky bacon and sliced sausage, then chopped pepper. Drain potatoes and add to the pan. Stir and add tomatoes. Cook for 5 minutes. Add peas. Spread the mixture either into little earthenware ramekins, or a wide, flat ovenproof dish and bake in a medium oven until the eggs have just solidified, but the yolks remain soft. The mixture minus the eggs can be prepared in advance and stored in the fridge or freezer.
(Kirsty Burrell)

BOLETUS (OR MUSHROOM) BURGERS

Any mushrooms can be used in this recipe, but the nutty flavour of the boletus complements the other ingredients. The burgers are excellent served with a yogurt and mayonnaise sauce, baked potatoes and a crunchy salad.

8oz(225g) mushrooms
1 medium onion
1 tablespoon flour
5fl oz(150ml) water
2oz(50g) ground nuts
1 tablespoon lemon juice
1 teaspoon yeast extract or mushroom ketchup
either nutmeg or garam masala to taste
6oz(175g) fresh wholewheat breadcrumbs
2 eggs, one of which is hard boiled
cooking oil

Finely chop the onion and mushrooms and fry in oil over a low heat until the onions are just beginning to brown and the mushrooms are tender. Stir in the flour, water, nuts, lemon juice and seasoning. Cook gently for 2-3 minutes then remove from heat and add 4oz(100g) of the breadcrumbs and the finely chopped boiled egg. Allow the mixture to cool, then shape into burgers; dip each one in beaten egg then coat with the remaining breadcrumbs. Fry in a hot pan until they are crisp and golden.
(Tess Darwin)

CHICKEN IN OYSTER SAUCE

1 large chicken with giblets
1 small onion
2 cloves garlic
3oz(75g) butter
black pepper and salt
Sauce:
1 dozen oysters
1 tablespoon cornflour
5fl oz(150ml) cream
1 tablespoon lemon juice
pepper and salt
watercress

Chop onion and garlic and fry in butter until clear. Joint the chicken and place in an ovenproof dish. Simmer the giblets in water to make a stock. Pour the butter, onions and garlic over the chicken, season with plenty of freshly ground black pepper and salt then place in a preheated oven at 375°F (190°C, mark 5). Baste from time to time. Open the oysters, carefully saving all the juices. When the chicken is cooked (about three quarters of an hour) take the chicken pieces out of the dish and keep warm. Remove excess fat off the chicken gravy and put the gravy in a pot. Add a little stock and then stir in the cornflour, mixed with a little water, to thicken. Gradually add lemon juice, and juice from oysters, continually stirring. Season to taste. Simmer for a few seconds, stir in the cream. Drop oysters into pan, bring to boil and remove from heat. Arrange chicken on a large dish, cover with oyster sauce, garnish with watercress.

(Sandra Macpherson)

GRILLED BREAST OF WOODPIGEON WITH WARM CUMBERLAND SAUCE

2 pigeon breasts per person
4oz(100g) potato per person
2oz(50g) shredded red cabbage
(cooked with a little grated apple and red wine)
1 orange
4 baby turnips per person
Sauce:
¼ bottle red wine
2fl oz(50ml) cider vinegar
2 finely chopped shallots
juice & zest of 2 oranges
juice of lemon
2 tablespoons redcurrant jelly
1oz(25g) English mustard
4fl oz(100ml) port wine

Reduce wine and vinegar by half. Add shallots, oranges and lemon juice and jelly, bring to the boil, skim, allow to cool, add mustard, the zest of 2 oranges finely shredded and blanched and wine. Allow the sauce to rest for 24 hours.

Peel the potatoes, shred them finely and place them into a small frying pan, which has been heated with a little oil and butter; fry the potatoes on each side until golden brown.

Season the breasts of woodpigeon (skins off), brush with clarified butter then place them on a hot charcoal grill allowing approximately 2 minutes each side. Peel and boil the baby turnips.

To serve: place the potato on a plate, then the cooked red cabbage, on top of the cabbage place the grilled breasts of woodpigeon. Coat the pigeon with warm Cumberland sauce and garnish with orange segments, zest and baby turnips rolled in butter.

(Graham Newbould)

BREASTS OF PIGEON WRAPPED IN BRUSSELS SPROUT LEAVES SERVED WITH A WILD RICE PANCAKE AND A MADEIRA SAUCE

Serves 4
4 pigeons
half an onion
half a carrot
1 onion cut into small cubes
1 carrot cut into small cubes
half a leek
2 cloves garlic
1 teaspoon celeriac
1 dessertspoon tomato puree
1 teaspoon sugar
2½ pints(1.5 litres) chicken stock
Bouquet garni:
crushed peppercorns
half a bayleaf
sprig of thyme
sliced green of leek
½ teaspoon crushed juniper berries
measure of madeira
For wild rice pancake:
7½ fl oz(250ml) cream and milk
5oz`(125g) plain flour
1 egg
1 egg yolk
1 egg white beaten separately
2oz(50g) cooked wild rice
The vegetables
12 turned carrots
12 turned courgettes
12 turned celeriac
24 mangetout
For the stuffing:
8oz(200g) chicken breast
8oz(200g) double cream
1oz(20g) egg white
salt and pepper
12oz(300g) large Brussels sprouts
(use outer leaves only)

Season the pigeons with salt and freshly ground pepper. Roast in a preheated oven 475°F (240°C, mark 9) for approximately one minute on each side. Place on a wire rack and cool.

Season and mince the chicken breasts and over bowl containing ice stir in the egg white. Pass the stuffing through a fine sieve into another bowl and add the chilled cream and re-season.

To prepare the stock, brown the *mirepoix* of onion and carrot in oil, then add the leek, celeriac and garlic and cook for a further minute. Stir in the tomato puree and sugar. Swill out the pan with water until there is a good brown basis. Pour in the chicken stock and bring to the boil.

Remove the pigeon breasts and chop the carcasses. Roast them with a little carrot and onion until golden brown. Drain, then add to the stock. Skim well and simmer gently for 2 hours, before adding the *bouquet garni*.

Prepare the Brussels sprouts by removing the larger leaves. Wash well. Then blanch in boiling salt water, refresh and drain on a cloth.

Cook the pigeon breasts with the chicken stuffing and lay on the brussels sprout leaves. Wrap the breasts in buttered greaseproof paper.

Prepare the vegetables. Cook them and refresh in cold water.

Wash the wild rice, simmer gently for approx 40-45 minutes. Refresh in cold water. Mix the cream and the milk together, beat in the flour, egg and egg yolk. Season and pass through a fine sieve and fold in the lightly beaten egg white.

Strain the pigeon stock after 3 hours and reduce by two-thirds. Thicken if necessary with a little cornflour. Stir in the measure of madeira, re-season and whisk in a knob of butter. Pan-fry the pigeon breasts in clarified butter for approximately 4-5 minutes. Grease 4 small cylindrical cutters. Spoon in the pancake batter. Sprinkle with a teaspoon of wild rice and fry. Trim and finish under the grill. (Mark Salter)

ROAST GOOSE AND GOOSEBERRY SAUCE

1 6-8lb(2.7-3.6kg) goose plus giblets
cooked wild rice
1 onion
1 cooking apple
3oz(75g) stoned dates
3oz(75g) dried apricots (soaked overnight)
1 teaspoon dried sage (or bunch of fresh)
1 tablespoon lemon juice
pepper and salt
3 tablespoons butter
1 glass port
1 tablespoon flour
sauce:
8oz(225g) gooseberries
2 tablespoons soft brown sugar
5fl oz(150ml) water

Chop the onion finely and grate the cooking apple. Boil the goose giblets (except liver) to make a stock for gravy. Halve the dates and chop the apricots and liver. Mix them together with onion, apple, sage, lemon juice and enough rice to fill the goose. Season the stuffing and also rub the inside of the bird with salt and pepper. Then put stuffing into the cavity. Rub pepper and salt over the skin and spread 2 tablespoons butter over the top. Place in roasting tin and put into preheated oven at 375°F (190°C, mark 5). Baste the bird occasionally and turn oven down to 350°F (180°C, mark 4) half way through cooking. It will take about 12-15 minutes per 1lb(450g). Ten minutes before bird is cooked, take out of the oven and remove excess fat. Pour over the top and place back into the oven to make the skin crisp. When ready lift bird out on to a hot serving dish. Mix flour into roasting tin and add stock from giblets to make gravy.

Put the gooseberries, brown sugar and water in a pan and cook until soft. Serve hot or cold with the roast.

(Sandra Macpherson)

QUAIL WITH PISTACHIO AND HERB STUFFING

4 quail
12oz(350g) white breadcrumbs
1 cup chopped pistachio nuts
3 leaves of fresh basil or parsley or lovage
1 rind of lemon
1 egg
2oz(50g) butter
honey to glaze

Mix the above ingredients and stuff the quail. Put 1oz(25g) butter on top and under the quail and place on a tray in a hot oven for 5-7 minutes. Remove and pour a large dessertspoon of honey over each quail. Return to the oven for 1 minute.

(Peter Jukes)

GAME PIE

1 grouse
1 partridge
2 pigeons
8oz(225g) sheep kidneys
3oz(75g) flour
2 onions
2 cloves garlic
2 carrots
4oz(100g) mushrooms
2oz(50g) butter
few sprigs tarragon
black pepper and salt
1 glass port
5fl oz(150ml) double cream
For rough puff pastry:
8oz(225g) plain flour
5oz(150g) margarine
2oz(50g) lard
pinch salt
2 teaspoons lemon juice
5fl oz(150ml) cold water
1 egg for glaze

Skin game and remove the meat from the bone. Slice the kidneys, cut the rest of the meat into pieces and toss in two thirds of the flour. Chop onion and garlic finely and fry in butter, in a large pot, for a few minutes. Add meat turning quickly to brown on all sides. Add sliced carrots and enough water to cover all ingredients. Season with pepper and salt, and bring to boil. Place lid on top of the pan and gently simmer for about 1½ hours or until meat is tender. Slice the mushrooms and add to the pot during the last few minutes of cooking. While the meat is cooking prepare the pastry. Cut the fat into small ½"(1cm) cubed pieces and drop into sieved flour and salt. Add lemon juice and water mixing together with a knife. Do not break up the pieces of fat.

Turn this onto a floured board and roll out into a rectangle. Fold top third down and bottom third up over the pastry.

Turn this around 90 degrees so that the folds are at the side and press them together. Roll and fold in this way four times. Wrap in foil and place in the fridge for half an hour.

Lift the meat and vegetables out of its gravy and place in a pie dish. Pour cream and port over the meat and then add enough of its gravy to just cover it, without being too full. Crush tarragon over the top and allow to cool. Roll out the pastry and cover dish. Brush the top of the pastry with egg (beaten with a little salt) make a little slit in the top and place pie in oven preheated to 425°F (220°C, mark 7) for about half an hour or until pastry is cooked and crisp.

(Sandra Macpherson)

ROAST PHEASANT WITH CELERY AND WALNUT STUFFING

½ hen pheasant per person
rashers of bacon
Stuffing: serves 4 to 6
4oz(100g) coarse-chopped walnuts
2 sticks of chopped celery
6oz(175g) finely chopped onion
2oz(50g) butter
3oz(75g) fresh breadcrumbs
1 tablespoon lemon juice
fine grated rind of half a lemon
1 egg
salt, pepper and nutmeg
¼ pint(150ml) red wine
¼ pint(150ml water)
1 dessertspoon flour

Cook the onions in butter until transparent, remove from heat and mix in the rest of the ingredients. Wash the pheasants and fill with the stuffing mixture. Place them in a roasting tin with the red wine and water. Push the legs well down the side of the birds and secure well with skewers. Sprinkle with salt and pepper and lightly smear with a little butter, particularly on the breasts and legs. Lay a rasher of bacon across each bird and cover with tin foil. Roast in a medium oven, 350°F (180°C, mark 4) for about an hour (15 minutes more for large birds). Baste twice during cooking and remove the foil and bacon for the last 10 minutes. Take the birds out of the tin and keep in a warm oven.

To make the gravy, whisk one dessertspoonful of flour into the juices in the pan. Add a little more red wine if this is too thick. Check the seasoning. Serve with Scots Potatoes.

BAKED HAM

The ideal meat for the Christmas sideboard. It is delicious hot or cold, and keeps well. It is easier to carve boned, but looks better with the bone in - you can decorate it with a paper frill.

1 gammon
1 large bottle of cider
8oz(225g) brown sugar
2 tablespoons whole grain mustard
1oz(25g) whole cloves

Soak the gammon overnight. Put it in a large, heavy-based pan, add the cider and top up with water to cover. Bring slowly to the boil, then simmer gently for 20 minutes for each 1lb(450g). Allow to cool in the cooking liquid. Take out the ham, reserving the liquid (freeze it in waxed juice cartons - enough stock for lentil soup for months). Carefully peel off the skin and score the fat in a diamond pattern. Stud with whole cloves in the intersections and pat a mixture of brown sugar and mustard over the surface. Roast in a hot oven 400°F (200°C, mark 6) for half an hour to glaze.

(Kirsty Burrell)

CROWN ROAST LAMB AND SKIRLIE

2 best end necks of lamb
1oz(25g) melted butter
pepper and salt
1lb(450g) plums
juice of half a lemon
2oz(50g) sugar
1 tablespoon water
8oz(225g) oatmeal (approx)
1 onion
2oz(50g) shredded suet
1 small bunch mint
black grapes
watercress

Make sure that the best end necks have been prepared by the butcher. Cut halfway down between each bone to separate cutlets. Take off about 1"(2cm) of the fat from the top of the bones. With the skin side inside curve both pieces round to make a crown. Stitch sides together. Cover bare tops of the bones with foil, brush the lamb with butter and season with pepper and salt. Place meat in a roasting tin in the centre of oven preheated to 425°F (220°C, mark 7) and roast for 15 minutes before turning heat down to 325°F (160°C, mark 3). Roast for roughly 20 minutes to 1lb(450g) and 20 minutes over, basting from time to time.

The Skirlie:
When roast is almost ready, take out about 2fl oz(50ml) of the fat from the roasting tin. Place suet in frying pan along with the roast fat. Chop onion finely and fry it in the fat adding enough oatmeal to absorb the fat. Stir well adding chopped mint. Fry for about 10-15 minutes.

Stone the plums and place in a pan with lemon juice and sugar. Simmer gently until soft.

Place roast on serving dish and remove foil. Fill the centre with skirlie and then pile the plums on top, reserving juice for sauce. Slit grapes, remove pips then cap each bone with a grape. Garnish with plenty of watercress around the base of joint.

Take off any excess fat from roasting dish and stir in a little hot water. Place over heat and add plum juice. Boil rapidly, thicken if desired or serve as it is with the roast.

(Sandra Macpherson)

SCOTTISH SPRING LAMB WITH SAVOY CABBAGE

Serves 4
4 cutlets of lamb 4-5oz(100-150g) well trimmed of all fat (clean bone well)
2fl oz(50ml) oil
1 bunch basil
2oz(50g) mixed vegetables (leeks, carrots, celery) in fine strips
4fl oz(100ml) dry sherry
1 pint(600ml) good veal or lamb stock of good brown colour
2oz(50g) unsalted butter
1 shallot or small onion finely chopped
1 small Savoy cabbage finely sliced
1oz(25g) chopped onion
1oz(25g) diced bacon
11/2 pints(900ml) whipping cream
sprig thyme and rosemary
nutmeg, salt, pepper

Cabbage:
Take the diced Savoy cabbage, onion, bacon and 1oz(25g) of butter. Sweat off the above ingredients for 5-7 minutes, without browning. Add the cream and reduce until of good consistency, not too thick. Season with salt and pepper. Keep warm.

Meat:
Season the lamb cutlets with salt and pepper, pan fry in a pan with a little oil slowly for about 7-9 minutes depending on how pink or well done you like them. Remove the cutlets from the pan and remove excess fat. Deglaze the pan with the sherry. Add the finely chopped shallot and the stock. Reduce the liquid until you have about ½ pint(300ml) left.

Pass the sauce through a muslin cloth or fine sieve into another pan. Add the fine vegetables, chopped basil and 1oz(25g) of butter. Whisk the butter into the sauce and warm thoroughly (don't boil).

Arrange the Savoy cabbage on the serving dish and dress the lamb on top. Place the sprigs of herbs on top and flash under the grill. Mask the sauce over the top and serve immediately with new potatoes or an orange and endive salad. (Charles Price)

RACK OF LAMB

A rack of lamb is sometimes called best end of lamb. The back bone is removed, the fat trimmed and the joint neatly tied, so that only the eight chops or cutlets are left with their bones. It makes a neat, easily carved little joint.

1lb(450g) potatoes
1 onion
2 cloves garlic
thyme and parsley

Brown the meat lightly and put in a casserole on a bed of sliced potatoes seasoned and layered with very thinly sliced onions and finely chopped garlic. Cover with foil and bake at 375°F (190°C, mark 5) for 50 minutes, then remove foil and cook for another 10 minutes. The juices from the meat can be drained off and added to a purée of haricot beans. (Kirsty Burrell)

BEST END OF LAMB TOPPED WITH WILD MUSHROOMS SERVED WITH MADEIRA SAUCE

Serves 4
1 or 2 small best ends of lamb (12 cutlets)
8oz(225g) chanterelles
1 small onion
2oz(50g) white breadcrumbs
seasoning
butter
For the sauce:
1 pint(600ml) lamb stock
3fl oz(75ml) Madeira
1fl oz(25ml) red wine
2 finely chopped shallots
a little fresh thyme
oil

Get the butcher to trim and cut the lamb into cutlets. Place the onion in the food processor and purée, then add the wild mushrooms and purée those. Melt the butter in a pan, add the mushroom purée and cook slowly, then add the breadcrumbs and check the seasoning. Heat the oil in a pan till it is smoking, then seal the lamb in the pan. Place on a tray and allow to cool. Top with the mousse. Sweat the thyme and shallots in a little butter, add the Madeira and red wine, reduce by half, add the lamb stock and reduce. While this is reducing return the lamb to the oven. When the stock is reduced by at least half, stir in about 2oz(50g) butter, do not reboil. Spoon a little on to each of the 4 plates and place cutlets on top. (Peter Jackson)

MARINATED BEEF FILLET, WITH A TIMBALE OF WILD RICE, RESTING ON A WOODLAND MUSHROOM PORT WINE SAUCE

Serves 4
1½lb(672g) trimmed beef fillet
For the marinade:
2½fl oz(65ml) olive oil
2 tablespoons port wine vinegar
2 tablespoons white vinegar
2½fl oz(65ml) soya sauce
12 juniper berries
16 mixed peppercorns
2½fl oz(65ml) port wine
2oz(56g) finely chopped onion
For the sauce:
2oz(56g) diced carrot, onion, celery
2oz(56g) butter
5fl oz(150ml) marinade
1 measure of port wine
10fl oz(300ml) brown veal stock (slightly thickened)
2oz(56g) black trumpets
2oz(56g) oyster mushrooms
2oz(56g) chanterelles
seasoning
For the timbale:
4oz(112g) Uncle Ben rice
1oz(28g) finely chopped onion
1oz(28g) butter
10fl oz(300ml) veal stock
1oz(28g) stick rice

Remove any fat and sinews from the beef fillet. Eye of meat should be 2" x 7"(5cm x 18cm). Mix all marinade ingredients together, place in tray with beef fillet and marinate for 24 hours, turning every six hours.

Heat copper pan with a little oil. Season beef with crushed peppercorns and salt; seal till golden brown. Cook in moderate

109

oven at 375°F (190°C, mark 5) till beef is cooked pink (approximately 6 minutes). Remove from oven, allow to rest and keep warm.

For the sauce, sweat down in a little butter onions, carrots and celery. Add marinade and port wine, reduce by half, add veal stock and further reduce to the correct consistency. Pass the sauce through fine strainer into clean bowl.

Lightly cook oyster mushrooms, trumpets and chanterelles for 30 seconds, add sauce. Bring to first boil; finish with hard butter; keep warm and cover with cling film. For the timbale, melt butter with onions, add rice, mix well and add veal stock; cover with greased greaseproof paper; cook in oven at 375°F (190°C, mark 5) for 17 minutes; mix through 1oz(28g) butter; keep warm in bowl.

Simmer stick rice in veal stock for 25-30 minutes. Add to above and mix together.

Put wild rice in 4 greased timbales, heat through in oven for 2 minutes. Turn out wild rice timbales onto 4 separate plates. Cut the beef fillet into 12 even slices, place at the side of each timbale. Bring sauce to boil and pour the woodland mushroom sauce around each portion. (Bill Gibb)

PICNIC BEEF

The cut of beef sold by Scottish butchers as fishtail is ideal (and cheap) for making this dish which can be eaten hot, but is at its best cold, as the centrepiece of a buffet or picnic meal. It should be prepared the day before.

1 piece of fishtail
4oz(100g) smoked streaky bacon
6 cloves garlic
4 tablespoons oil
2 onions
small wine glass of brandy
2 large carrots
thyme, bay leaves
1 calf's foot or 2 pigs trotters
10fl oz(300ml) wine (red or white)
stock

Lard the meat with the bacon cut into strips and chips of garlic and rub with a little salt and ground pepper. Saute the onions in the oil then put in the meat and brown all over. Warm the brandy

in a soup ladle, pour it over the meat and set light to it. When the flames have died down transfer to a deep casserole. Add the carrots, the calf's foot or trotters and the herbs and enough stock or water to barely cover. Simmer very gently on top of the stove or in the oven for 4 hours. The beef can be served hot, surrounded by carrots cooked separately in beef stock, with the reduced cooking liquor as a sauce.

Otherwise let the meat cool in the liquid for 3 hours, then remove it to a close-fitting dish. Reduce the stock a little by boiling it, strain it over the meat. Leave in the fridge overnight. Next day, when the stock has set, remove the fat from the surface. The whole thing can be turned out onto an ashet or large serving dish. If you line the dish in which the meat is to be left to set with fresh herbs and carrots (cooked separately), when you turn it out they will be set in clear jelly. (Kirsty Burrell)

HALLOWE'EN STEW

A really hearty stew, perfect for cold, hungry guisers. Serve it in a large pumpkin shell. The ingredients are all flexible.

1lb(450g) chick peas (soaked overnight)
1lb(450g) stewing beef (in a piece)
1 ham shank
1 spicey cooking sausage, such as the Spanish chorizo
1 whole round of butcher's black pudding (optional)
4 heads of sweetcorn
1lb(450g) pumpkin
½ sliced cabbage (Savoy)
2 sweet potatoes
4 potatoes
1lb(450g) green beans
4 pears
2 cloves garlic
1 teaspoon nutmeg, salt and pepper

Drain the chick peas and put them in a large pot with all the meat (not cut up) and cover with water. Bring to the boil, skim and simmer on top of the stove or in the oven for 1½ hours. Check that the chick peas are softening - if not give them a bit longer. Add the whole sweetcorn. Over the next hour gradually add the cabbage, the sweet potatoes, peeled and cut up, the pumpkin, cubed (it will dissolve and thicken the stew) the potatoes, scrubbed and sliced roughly, the pears, quartered and peeled and last of all the green beans, topped and tailed. Crush the garlic with the salt, pepper and nutmeg and stir it into the stew. At this point transfer the stew to the hollowed-out pumpkin shell, first removing the meat, taking the ham off the bone and chopping all the meat into bite-sized pieces and also chopping the sweetcorn into 2"(5cm) lengths. Put the stew, inside the pumpkin shell, into an ovenproof dish for safety and leave in a low oven until needed.
(Kirsty Burrell)

ROAST SADDLE OF ROE DEER WITH APPLE PUREE AND ROSEMARY SAUCE

Allow:
6-8oz(175-225g) meat per person (boned)
10-12oz(275-350g) on the bone
¼ bottle red wine
5fl oz(150ml) game or veal stock
1oz(25g) butter
good bunch of fresh rosemary
1 cooking apple purée
1 cooking apple for garnish (cooked in water, butter and sugar)
onion, celery, leek and carrot
Marinade:
½ bottle red wine
1 carrot
1 leek
1 onion
1 stick celery
18 juniper berries crushed
boil together and allow to cool
zest of 1 lemon
2 cloves
1 tablespoon redcurrant jelly

Take 12oz(350g) roe deer saddle on the bone, remove the eye of the meat from the bone, remove any sinew from the meat, keep the bones. Marinade the meat for 24 hours.

To make the sauce: roast the bones until brown, tip off any excess fat, add a little chopped onion, carrot, leek and celery, and allow them to brown (be careful not to burn the vegetables because it will turn the sauce bitter). Add ¼ bottle of red wine and a good bunch of rosemary and reduce to 1 tablespoon syrup consistency, add a little of the marinade and reduce again. To this add 5fl oz(150ml) game or veal stock and reduce by a half. Strain the sauce, correct the seasoning and beat in 1oz(25g) butter to finish.

Apple purée:

Allow 1 apple per person peeled and pipped, sweat the apple in a little butter with 1oz(25g) brown sugar, a sprig of rosemary, 2 cloves and juice of ¼ lemon. When cooked pass the apple through a fine sieve to make the purée.

To cook the meat: take the meat from the marinade salt and pepper place it in a hot pan; with a little oil and butter and roast it in the oven for approximately 5 minutes. Remove the meat from the pan and allow it to rest for 5 minutes, then slice the meat thinly; arrange it on a warm plate, cover the meat with a little sauce served with a quenelle of apple purée and cooking apple garnish (cooked whole in water, butter and sugar and turned frequently). (Graham Newbould)

LOIN OF RABBIT WRAPPED IN SCHUPFNUDELN WITH A PORT WINE SAUCE

Serves 4
2 rabbits 2¼lb(1kg) each
For the stock:
2 onions
2 carrots
½ leek
2 cloves garlic
1 teaspoon celeriac
1 dessertspoon tomato purée
1 teaspoon sugar
2¼ pints(1½ litres) chicken stock (or 2 stock cubes)
For the bouquet garni:
crushed white peppercorns
½ bayleaf
sprig of thyme
sliced green of leek
1 measure of port
selection of fresh vegetables
For the schüpfnüdeln:
1lb 4oz(500g) potatoes
4oz(100g) plain flour
1 egg & 1 egg yolk
1½oz(40g) butter
salt & pepper
nutmeg

Have the loins from both rabbits removed, season and fry in clarified butter. Leave to cool. Use remaining rabbit for a casserole or a stuffing. Roast the chopped rabbit carcasses.

Stock: in a saucepan brown the cubes of carrot and onion in oil Add the leek, garlic and celeriac. Mix in the tomato purée and sugar. Brown slowly and swill out with water three times browning the stock basis a little more each time. Pour in the chicken stock. Bring to the boil, add the rabbit carcasses and skim. Simmer gently adding the bouquet garni after 1½ hours. For the schüpfnüdeln: cook the potatoes in salt water, drain and dry out in the oven for 5-10 minutes. Mash the potatoes and pass through a potato press onto the knobs of butter. Cool. Mix in the beaten egg and egg yolk. Add the flour and season.

Wrap the loins of rabbit in the schüpfnüdeln then fry gently in clarified butter for about 10 minutes.

Strain the stock and boil until only 5fl oz(150ml) remains. Finish with a measure of port and knobs of butter.

Serve with compote of leek with oranges. (Mark Salter)

POTATO CAKES

oil
potatoes
seasoning

Heat the oil in a frying pan. Peel and grate the potato; season. When the oil is just smoking, carefully put the grated potato and shape into a pancake shape. When golden brown turn over and when the other side is brown, place in a moderate oven for 10 minutes. (Peter Jackson)

SCOTS POTATOES

Slice medium-sized potatoes into rounds, dry them on kitchen paper, make an egg wash with one egg, 2fl oz(50ml) milk, salt and pepper, dip the potatoes in seasoned flour, then in the egg wash, then in medium oatmeal and finally fry them in deep fat for 8-10 minutes. (Helen Broughton)

POTATOES BAKED IN CREAM WITH GARLIC

4 large waxy potatoes (Desirée are excellent)
1 clove of garlic
salt and pepper
cream

Peel and finely slice the potatoes. Dry off the slices in a towel and put them in layers in a casserole with finely chopped garlic, salt and freshly ground pepper.
They should be about 1½"-2"(4cm-5cm) deep. Pour in cream to just cover potatoes. Cover with tinfoil and put in hot oven for about one hour.
Check after 20-30 minutes and if cooking nicely remove tinfoil and continue cooking at a low temperature until almost soft. The dish can be left covered in a warm place for 10-15 minutes before serving. (Betty Allen)

DULSE DOLLOPS

Seaweed and vegetable croquettes to be served as a side dish.

2oz(50g) dried dulse
4oz(100g) coarse oatmeal
1lb(450g) root vegetables: potatoes, swedes, turnips, parsnips, carrots
cooking oil

Boil the dulse and vegetables together until tender. Mash the mixture adding some of the cooking water if necessary, then thicken with oatmeal until it is of a handling consistency. Shape into small, flat croquettes and roll in the remaining oatmeal. Allow to firm in the fridge before frying in oil in a moderately hot pan until crisp, shaking and turning as necessary to prevent the oatmeal from burning.
(Tess Darwin)

COURGETTE TARTS

1 courgette
1 egg
2fl oz(50ml) double cream
seasoning
short pastry

Finely dice the courgette and season. Line four tart moulds with the short paste. Whisk the egg and double cream, season. Divide the courgette between the moulds and top up with egg custard. Bake in a moderate oven till golden brown. (Peter Jackson)

COMPOTE OF LEEK WITH ORANGES

2 large leeks
2oz(50g) butter
pinch of sugar
salt
orange fillets from 2 oranges

Finely slice the leeks, wash and cook slowly in butter, sugar, salt and finely diced garlic. Fillet the oranges and moisten the compote with a little orange juice. Use the orange fillets to garnish the top of the compote. (Mark Salter)

BROCCOLI AND WALNUT MOUSSE

2lb(900g) broccoli
2 egg whites
walnuts, roughly chopped
seasoning
butter for greasing the moulds

Trim any excess stalk off the broccoli, take 2 stalks and cut the florettes into small pieces, keep raw and separate. Place a large pan of water on to boil with plenty of salt. When boiling, throw in the broccoli and cook till soft. Purée in a food processor with the egg whites, fold in the raw broccoli and walnuts. Check seasoning.
Butter four small ramekins and fill with the mousse. Cover with tinfoil and make 2 little holes in it to let the steam out, or the steam will souffé the mousse.
Place in a moderate oven for 12-15 minutes. Remove the tin foil and run a knife round the edge and turn out. (Peter Jackson)

SUMMER FRUIT SORBETS AND ICE CREAM

Ice cream can be made with any well-flavoured fruit. For a change try damson, gooseberry or a combination of raspberries and redcurrants. Add the juice of an orange to strawberries, juice of half a lemon to raspberries. Harder fruits such as gooseberries should be cooked until soft first. The basic recipe for a water-ice is:

A syrup made boiling together 5 fl oz(150ml) water and 8oz(225g) sugar for 5 mins. (Cook slowly and stir until the sugar has dissolved, then rapidly.)
1 pint fruit purée
For fruit, which has to be cooked first, simply add the sugar to the fruit before cooking.
For ice cream add 5 fl oz(150ml) whipped cream.

Stir the ingredients together and freeze, covered with foil, stirring sides to middle a few times, for 2-3 hours. (Kirsty Burrell)

SUMMER FRUIT SOUP WITH BANANA MOUSSE

Serves 4
selection of available soft fruit:
(raspberries, loganberries, strawberries, brambles, red, white or black currants)
For the sauce:
8oz(225g) soft strawberries or any soft fruit
2oz(50g) icing sugar
1fl oz(25ml) Glayva
2fl oz(50ml) water
For banana mousse:
2 bananas
2oz(50g) melted butter
4fl oz(100ml) double cream
2oz(50g) icing sugar

Set aside fruit for decoration. Purée the remainder for the sauce, add the icing sugar and Glayva. Add the water till you get the correct sauce consistency. Pass through a sieve. Liquidise the bananas with the melted butter, add the cream and icing sugar. Liquidise for about another 30 seconds, place in a container and chill until set. Coat the plate with fruit sauce, decorate with soft fruit round it. Make quenelles out of the banana mousse and place in the middle or pipe in the middle. (Peter Jackson)

FESTIVE CASSATA

A pudding cake which is rich, but not too sweet, and can be decorated with chocolate flowers and leaves and candles. Make it in a heart-shaped mould or a pudding basin.

1lb(450g) ricotta or curd cheese
2oz(50g) sugar
1 small wine glass Drambuie
4oz(100g) mixed chopped candied peel
2oz(50g) bitter chocolate
1 packet sponge fingers
for icing:
6oz(175g) bitter chocolate
3oz(75g) butter
juice of half an orange

Beat together the cheese, the sugar and 2 tablespoons Drambuie. Chop the chocolate into small chips. Fold chocolate and candied peel into the cheese. Line the mould with foil (it's easier if you smooth it over the outside first). Soak the sponge fingers in the remaining Drambuie and line the mould with them. Fill with cheese mixture and cover with sponge fingers. Fold the foil over the top and leave in the fridge overnight. To make the icing, melt the chocolate with the orange juice on top of a double boiler. Off the heat, mix in the butter, chopped in small pieces, very gradually.
When the icing has cooled a little turn the cake out and spread on the icing. Return to the fridge for at least an hour. (Kirsty Burrell)

MARQUISE ALBA

Another pudding cake - suitable for grown-up birthdays or, made in a heart-shaped mould, for St Valentine's Day.

First bake a chocolate-flavoured Genoise sponge in the mould. Take it out and leave it on a cake rack.

To make the marquise:
1 teaspoon gelatine
12 fl oz(350ml) double cream
10oz(275g) white chocolate
1 fl oz(25ml) liquid glucose
(available from chemists)
3 egg yolks

Sprinkle the gelatine onto 3 tablespoons of hot water and stir until dissolved. Whip the cream. Mix the glucose with 2 fl oz(50ml) water and bring to the boil. Take off the heat add the chocolate broken into pieces and the gelatine. Stir until smooth. When the mixture is blood temperature add the beaten egg yolks and fold in the cream. Pour the mixture into the mould and refrigerate overnight. To unmould it, place the mould in very hot water for a few seconds, then turn out on top of the sponge. Decorate with dark chocolate flowers and leaves, purchased from a good confectioner.
(Kirsty Burrell)

RHUBARB MERINGUE TART

8oz(225g) flour
4 tablespoons caster sugar
3oz(75g) butter
1 egg yolk
1lb(450g) rhubarb
4oz(100g) caster sugar
1 tablespoon lemon juice
2 egg yolks
pinch cinnamon
3 egg whites
5 fl oz(150ml) double cream

Sieve the flour and 1 tablespoon of sugar into a bowl then rub in the butter until mixture resembles breadcrumbs. Mix an egg yolk into the dry ingredients adding a little water to make a firm dough. Roll out into a round. Butter a flan ring and a baking sheet. Place the ring on top of the sheet then line with dough.

Chop the rhubarb into small pieces and put them into a pot with 4oz(100g) caster sugar, lemon juice and pinch of cinnamon. Simmer gently until almost tender. Take off the heat and allow to cool. Strain off excess juice and keep this for serving with the tart. Stir the two egg yolks into the rhubarb then pile mixture into lined flan ring. Bake in oven Gas 400°F (200°C, mark 6) for about 20 minutes until tart is cooked. Turn oven down to 250°F (120°C, mark ½). Remove the ring and leave tart on baking sheet. Whip the 3 egg whites until stiff. Fold into 3 tablespoons sieved caster sugar and spread meringue mixture on top of tart completely sealing the fruit. Place in the cool oven and bake until meringue is hard. This tart can be served hot or cold with whipped cream and the remaining juice from fruit.
(Sandra Macpherson)

RUM AND NUTTY PUDDING

For the biscuits:
2oz(50g) butter
2oz(50g) sugar
3oz(75g) self raising flour
rind of 1 lemon
3oz(75g) nuts (walnuts or hazelnuts)
To finish:
black rum
cream
soft brown sugar

Cream butter and sugar together and add the flour. Add the lemon rind and nuts and mix well. Shape into walnut sized rounds and bake at 350°F (180°C, mark 4). Place nut biscuits on dish, soak with black rum. Whip cream and fold in dark soft brown sugar and spread on top. (Peter Jukes)

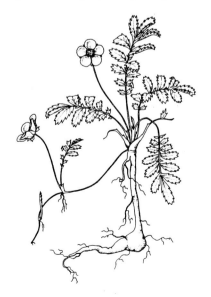

115

CRANACHAN CHOUX

Choux pastry:
7½ fl oz(215ml) water
3oz(75g) butter
3¾ oz(90g) plain flour
3 small eggs
2oz(50g) white chocolate

Put water and butter into pan and bring to boil. Take the pan off heat, allow bubbles to subside, then add sieved flour. Stir until smooth. Allow to cool for a few minutes. Beat the eggs with a fork, then gradually beat them into the mixture. Only add enough beaten egg to keep the mixture firm. Continue beating for a few minutes until it looks glossy. Preset the oven to 400°F (200°C, mark 6). Place spoonfuls of the mixture onto a greased oven sheet, making sure that there is about 3"(7cm) between each one, to allow them to expand. Bake for 20 minutes or until crisp. Lift them out on to a wire rack to cool and prick to release steam.

Cranachan:
½ pint(300ml) double cream
2oz(50g) coarse oatmeal
1 tablespoon caster sugar
4oz(100g) raspberries

Toast the oatmeal and allow to cool, whip the cream until stiff and sieve the sugar. Fold sugar and oatmeal into the cream then finally fold in the raspberries, reserving a few berries to decorate the dish.
Cut open the choux pastry and fill each one with cranachan. Melt the white chocolate and spoon a little over the tops. Arrange on an attractive serving dish. If the cranachan is put sparingly into the choux, then the remainder can be served separately in a small glass bowl.
(Sandra Macpherson)

BLAEBERRY TART

A traditional Highland recipe that can be made with any juicy berry if blaeberries are scarce.

1lb(450g) blaeberries
8oz(225g) dessert apples
12oz(350g) shortcrust pastry
sugar
lemon juice

Gently stew the blaeberries in minimal water for a few minutes (they are very juicy). Line an 8"(20cm) pie dish with half the pastry and bake blind for 10 minutes at 400°F (200°C, mark 6). Cover the pastry with thinly sliced apple (to absorb the blaeberry juice) then pour in the blaeberries. Sprinkle with sugar and lemon juice, then cover with remaining pastry. Bake for 25 minutes 350°F (180°C, mark 4).
(Tess Darwin)

BLAEBERRY PANCAKES

4oz(100g) plain flour
1/4 teaspoon salt
1 dessertspoon corn oil
1 egg
1/2 pint(300ml) milk
1 tablespoon melted butter
1lb(450g) blaeberries
4oz(100g) caster sugar
1 dessertspoon kirsch
1 dessertspoon cornflour
2oz(50g) icing sugar
5 fl oz(150ml) double cream

Sieve flour and salt. Mix to smooth batter with egg, corn oil and half the milk. Stir in the rest of the milk and allow to sit for 30 minutes. Melt a little butter in a large heavy pan and when hot pour some of the mixture into it, thinly covering the bottom. Fry until golden brown then turn and cook the other side. Continue process until all the batter is used.
Put blaeberries into a pan with sugar and kirsch and bring to a boil. Simmer gently until the fruit is tender. Drain fruit saving the juice. Spread some cooked berries over each pancake and roll them up. Heat for 10 minutes before serving and then dust with sieved icing sugar. Blend the cornflour with the blaeberry juice and cook until thickened. Serve this sauce with the filled pancakes. Also served whipped double cream if desired.
(Sandra Macpherson)

GLAZED APPLE PANCAKES WITH HONEY, WHISKY AND TOASTED OATMEAL ICE CREAM QUENELLES

Serves 6
7½fl oz(250ml) milk
6oz(150g) plain flour
4 eggs
pinch salt, sugar and cinnamon
6 strawberries
6 sprigs of mint
For the ice cream:
22½fl oz(750ml) milk
7½fl oz(250ml) cream
1 vanilla stick
10oz(250g) sugar
4 eggs
2 egg yolks
4oz(100g) toasted medium oatmeal
2 measures whisky
1 teaspoon honey

Mix the flour and milk together, add the salt, sugar and cinnamon. Whisk in the eggs and strain the batter through a fine sieve. Rest overnight. Prepare the ice cream by boiling the milk, then gradually mixing into the cream, over a saucepan of hot water. Stir the ice cream until it coats the back of a wooden spoon. Add the honey and whisky, then chill and turn in an ice cream maker. At the last moment, add the toasted medium oatmeal and freeze.

Peel and core the apples. Cut in half then into quarters. Slice about 4 wedges from each quarter and sprinkle with sugar. In a non-stick frying pan pour in a little clarified butter. Ladle in the pancake batter and arrange the apple around the perimeter. Sprinkle with more sugar and flip the pancake. Add a knob of fresh butter and cook until the apples have caramelised and the pancake is cooked. Turn out onto a plate and garnish with 3 quenelles of honey, whisky and toasted oatmeal ice cream, a few fresh strawberries and sprigs of mint. (Mark Salter)

CHESTNUT MIXTURE FOR PROFITEROLES

8oz(225g) tin chestnut purée (unsweetened)
1 tablespoon brandy(optional) or rum
2oz(50g) caster sugar
½pint(300ml) double cream

Beat together the chestnut purée, brandy and sugar. Whip the cream and fold it into the chestnut mixture. (Kirsty Burrell)

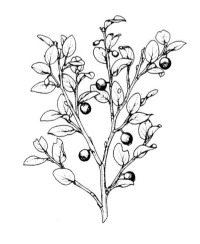

TEARS OF DARK CHOCOLATE FILLED WITH WHISKY MOUSSE

4oz(100g) dark bitter chocolate
For the whisky mousse:
1 egg
1 egg yolk
6oz(175g) dark bitter chocolate
2fl oz(50ml) whisky
5fl oz(150ml) double cream
For the chocolate sauce:
7fl oz(200ml) milk
4oz(100g) white chocolate
clear plastic strips,
8"x1"(20cm x 2cm)

Tears:
Melt the chocolate in a double boiler until smooth (approximately 46°-48°C). Carefully reheat it to 36°C.
Paint the chocolate on the flexible plastic strips nip the two ends together and make a tear shape, when the chocolate is set peel off the plastic.
Mousse:
Melt the chocolate in a double boiler, whisk the whole egg and ribbon consistency. Whisk the chocolate into the mixture at the same temperature.
Finally incorporate the lightly whipped cream to which the whisky has been added.
Allow the mousse to set and pipe the mousse into the tear shaped chocolate cases.
Serve the tears on a white chocolate sauce.
Sauce:
Bring the milk to the boil.
Remove from the heat and stir in the finely chopped white chocolate until smooth. Allow to cool. (Graham Newbould)

CLOUTIE DUMPLING

8oz(225g) plain flour
5oz(150g) shredded suet
6oz(175g) currants
6oz(175g) sultanas
4oz(100g) white breadcrumbs
1 teaspoon baking powder
1 grated apple
1 teaspoon cinnamon
1 teaspoon ginger
pinch salt
2oz(50g) brown sugar
2 tablespoons treacle
2 eggs
milk
3 tangerines
1 orange grated rind only
2oz(50g) caster sugar
1oz(25g) butter
1 egg
1 tablespoon orange liquor
5 fl oz(150ml) single cream

First scald a white linen cloth, allow it to cool then dust with flour. (This forms the skin). Mix all dry ingredients together. Dissolve the treacle in a little milk and eggs and add to the dry ingredients. Increase the amount of milk if necessary to make a soft dropping consistency. Pile this into the centre of the prepared cloth. Tie up with string leaving enough room for expansion. Place this on a plate in a large pot of boiling water, cover and simmer for 3 to 4 hours. Lift cloutie dumpling out of the water and dip in cold water for a few seconds to stop dumpling sticking to the cloth. Place in a bowl, untie cloth and then turn dumpling onto a large heated plate. To do this place the plate upside down over the bowl and turn over allowing pudding to drop out.

Peel tangerines and remove pips (if any), and make into a purée with a blender. Grate the orange. Place the caster sugar and butter in a double saucepan or in a bowl over hot water and stir until the sugar melts. Whisk the egg and add this to the mixture along with orange rind, stirring continuously. Stir in the tangerine purée and orange liquor and continue to stir until sauce thickens. Remove from heat, allow to cool then place in fridge. Serve the sauce cold with the dumpling and a small jug of single cream.

(Sandra Macpherson)

PUMPKIN PIE

Make with the inside of the pumpkin at Hallowe'en.

9"(23cm) sweet shortcrust pie shell, lightly baked blind
12fl oz(325ml) cooked pumpkin
4oz(100g) brown sugar
12fl oz(325ml) double cream
½ teaspoon cinnamon, nutmeg, pinch of allspice
½ teaspoon ginger
3 eggs
pecan nuts or walnuts (optional)

Steam pumpkin until soft. Drain off excess fluid and liquidise. Mix in sugar, spices, cream and eggs. Pour into pie shell, decorate with half pecans or walnuts and bake in a low oven 325°F (170°C, mark 3) until set (about an hour).

(Kirsty Burrell)

PEAR AND WHISKY SYLLABUB WITH SOFT WILD FRUITS

Serves 4
4 egg yolks
3oz(75g) caster sugar
4oz(100g) Greek style yogurt
1½ pints(900ml) whipping cream
4fl oz(100ml) Glendronach whisky sherry casked
raspberries
blueberries
strawberries
tayberries
brambles or any other soft fruits
4 sprigs mint

Beat the egg yolks and sugar over a hot water bath till ribbing stage. (This is when you start to leave the print of the whisk in the eggs. The water bath must be just warm not boiling). Add the yogurt to the eggs and sugar with the whisky. Fold through the whipped cream. The soft fruits can be folded through the mixture or layered when putting the syllabub into the goblets or glasses. Shortbread fingers can be served with this dish. (Charles Price)

CREAM CROWDIE

Usually made with raspberries, this simple but rich dessert can include any soft fruit.

8oz(225g) berries, any variety or mixed kinds
10fl oz(300ml) double cream
2oz(50g) rough oatmeal
2oz(50g) sugar

Toast the oatmeal carefully in a heavy pan. Whip the cream until thick. Stir all the ingredients together and serve. Can be chilled. (Tess Darwin)

CARAGHEEN CREAM

Based on a traditional Hebridean dish, this recipe uses chocolate and coffee to add flavour and mask any taste of the sea which might not appeal to the modern palate.

1 cup dried caragheen
3 cups milk
1 tablespoon sugar
1 tablespoon coffee granules
2oz(50g) dark cooking chocolate

Wash and soak the caragheen for 30 minutes. Simmer gently in the milk for about 20 minutes until thick. Add the sugar and coffee, stir well. Strain, then add the melted chocolate and beaten egg. Reheat without allowing to boil for 1-2 minutes. Pour into mould and leave to set. Serve with cream or natural yogurt.
(Tess Darwin)

POPPYSEED PARFAIT WITH BRAMBLE AND STRAWBERRY SAUCE

Serves 8
9oz(220g) caster sugar
6 whole eggs
7½ fl oz(250ml) milk
6oz(150g) poppyseeds
2 leaves gelatine
pinch of cinnamon
17oz(750g) lightly beaten cream
For the shortbread biscuit:
6oz(150g) plain flour
4oz(100g) butter
2oz(50g) sugar
5fl oz(150ml) double cream
grated chocolate to garnish
The sauce:
8oz(200g) brambles
8oz(200g) strawberries or raspberries
10fl oz(300ml) stock syrup
10fl oz(300ml) water
4oz(100g) sugar
squeeze of lemon juice

Beat the eggs and sugar over hot water until peaks are formed. Boil the milk and the poppyseeds together and stir in the soaked leaf gelatine. Mix the egg and milk mixture together and cool over ice before mixing in the pinch of cinnamon and the lightly beaten cream. Pour into moulds or small timbale forms and freeze for 2 hours.

Blend the fruits separately in a liquidiser and mix with a little stock syrup and a squeeze of lemon juice. Strain through a fine sieve.

Cream the butter and the sugar and mix in the sieved plain flour. Roll out the paste using flour and cut into rounds. Place on a tray and rest in the fridge before baking in the oven for 20-25 minutes. Leave the trays to cool sprinkling lightly with sugar as they leave the oven.

Ladle on the two sauces, place on a piece of shortbread and a slice of parfait cut out using a similar size cutter to the shortbread. Pipe on a little cream and garnish with chocolate.
(Mark Salter)

ALMOND COOKIE BASKET FILLED WITH DRAMBUIE ICE CREAM AND FRESH ORANGE ON A VANILLA SAUCE

Serves 4:
For the cookie basket:
2oz(56g) icing sugar
2oz(56g) egg white
¾oz(20g) melted butter
¾oz(20g) flour
½oz(14g) oil
1oz(28g) almond nibs
For the Drambuie parfait:
6 egg yolks
5oz(140g) sugar
6fl oz(175ml) milk
1 measure of Drambuie
10fl oz(300ml) double cream
For the vanilla sauce:
2 egg yolks
2oz(56g) sugar
10fl oz(300ml) milk
vanilla pod or essence
8oz(225g) skinned orange segments
1oz(28g) icing sugar

For the cookie basket:
Mix egg white, sugar and flour together, beat until smooth. Add melted butter and oil, continue to beat and pass through strainer into a clean bowl.

Thinly coat 4 circles on greased non-stick tray, approximately 4"(10cm) diameter. Sprinkle with almond nibs. Cook at 375°F (190°C, mark 5) until golden brown. Remove from tray with palette knife, shape over small mould or inverted cups immediately to form basket, while paste is still warm.
For the parfait:
Cream together egg yolks, sugar and Drambuie. Gradually add hot milk. Return to clean pan, cook until mixture coats the back of spatula (do not boil). Pass through strainer into clean bowl, place on ice until cool. Lightly whip cream, fold into Drambuie base. Place in plastic bowl and freeze

Warm milk and vanilla pod together. Cream egg yolks and sugar. Gradually add milk, return to clean saucepan; cook until mixture coats the back of spatula; pass through strainer, sprinkle lightly with sugar. Allow to cool. Cut the orange segments in half. Pour a little sauce into the centre of each plate. Fill basket with Drambuie ice cream and fresh oranges. Place on sauce and decorate round the basket with 4 half segments. (Bill Gibb)

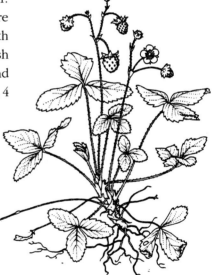

SPRING LEMON CAKE

A simple, fresh-tasting cake, particularly easy to make in a food processor.

grated rind of 1 lemon
6oz(175g) caster sugar
8oz(225g) unsalted butter cut in pieces
4 eggs
8oz(225g) self raising flour
1 level teaspoon baking powder
pinch of salt
2 tablespoons lemon juice
For the syrup:
juice of 1 lemon
4oz(100g) granulated sugar
for decoration:
angelica, crystallised mimosa

If using a food processor put all the ingredients in the bowl and mix till smooth. Otherwise beat butter, sugar and lemon rind together, beat in eggs and lemon juice and fold in flour, baking powder and salt. Turn into an 8"(20cm) loose-bottomed cake tin, lined with bakewell paper and bake at 350°F (180°C, mark 4) for 1¼ hours, or until the cake is pale golden and slightly shrunk from the sides of the tin and springs back when pressed with a finger in the centre. While the cake is baking stir together the sugar and lemon juice. When the cake comes out of the oven decorate it while still in the tin with 'sprigs' of angelica and mimosa, then spoon the lemon syrup over it. Leave in the tin till all the syrup has soaked in and the cake has cooled before lifting out carefully. (Kirsty Burrell)

GILDED GINGERBREAD

A good alternative to Christmas cake. Bake it, perhaps, in a Christmas tree-shaped tin and decorate with runny green-tinted glacé icing and silver and gold-coated sugared almonds, or bake in a loaf tin and try gilding it with the thin sheets of silver tissue known as 'vark' obtainable in some Indian grocers, or simply decorate with crystallised ginger.

1lb(450g) plain flour
1 teaspoon bicarbonate of soda
1 teaspoon baking powder
½ teaspoon salt
1½ teaspoons ground ginger
1 teaspoon ground cloves
1 teaspoon cinnamon
6oz(175g) unsalted butter
8oz(225g) soft brown sugar
16oz(450g) black treacle & syrup
2 eggs
½ pint(300ml) milk
2oz(50g) citron peel
4oz(100g) crystallised ginger
2oz(50g) pine nuts
2oz(50g) slivered almonds

Butter tin and dust with flour. Sift together flour, bicarb, baking powder, salt and spices. Warm the butter, sugar, treacle and syrup in a pan over low heat until the butter has just melted. Stir the melted ingredients into the centre of the dry mixture then beat in the milk and beaten egg. Fold in the chopped peel and ginger, and the nuts. Bake in a slow oven 325°F (170°C, mark 3) for 1½ hours, until well risen and firm to the touch. Leave to cool for 15 minutes in tin, then turn out onto a cake rack. This cake keeps well in an airtight tin, in fact it should be made at least a week before eating.
(Kirsty Burrell)

RICH WARM CHOCOLATE GATEAU

1 dessertspoon instant coffee
4 tablespoons hot water
14oz(400g) chocolate
2oz(50g) unsweetened cocoa powder
2 tablespoons dark rum
6 large eggs
4oz(100g) caster sugar
8fl oz(225ml) double cream
1 dessertspoon vanilla essence

Line the bottom of a 9"(23cm) non-stick tin with bakewell paper. Set bowl over pot of hot water (not boiling). Put water in bowl and dissolve coffee, add broken chocolate, sifted cocoa powder and rum. Leave to melt. Beat eggs and sugar until the mixture has reached the consistency of lightly whipped cream. Whip cream and vanilla only to soft peaks. When chocolate has melted beat lightly with a wooden spoon - it should be smooth. Fold chocolate into egg mixture quickly and lightly; when partially incorporated fold in cream till just combined. Pour into tin and place in *bain marie* containing warm water. Bake for 1¼ hours at 350°F (18°0C, Mark 4). Turn off oven and leave in oven with door open for half an hour. Remove from oven and leave in *bain marie* for half an hour. When cool remove from tin. Reheat gently for about half an hour in a low oven and serve warm. (Betty Allen)

SILVERWEED BANNOCKS

A very old recipe for a characteristically Scottish dish; the roots should only be collected where the plant is very common (or better still from your own garden). Like ordinary oatcakes, these bannocks are delicious with butter and cheese, or spread with jam or honey.

4oz(100g) young silverweed roots (best in March and April)
4oz(100g) oatmeal
½ teaspoon salt
2oz(50g) melted butter
milk or water
fine oatmeal or wholewheat flour for rolling

Wash the roots and dry for several hours in the sun, airing cupboard or warming oven. Reduce the roots to flour in a coffee grinder. Mix the flour with the oatmeal and salt, then stir in the butter. Add sufficient milk or water to make a stiff paste, then knead well. Roll out to ½"(1cm) thick, shape into a circle using a dinner plate then cut into quarters. Cook slowly on a bannock slab or thick bottomed pan until well browned, then turn and cook the other side. Alternatively it can be baked in a moderate oven for about 20 minutes. (Tess Darwin)

ORANGE AND GRAND MARNIER TERRINE

Segments from 8 oranges
8oz(225g) caster sugar
½ pint(300ml) water
1½ tablespoons Grand Marnier
rind of 2 oranges blanched in boiling water
½oz(10g) gelatine

Dissolve the sugar in the water. Allow liquid to cool then sprinkle in gelatine and leave until dissolved. Add Grand Marnier. Line the bottom of a 9" x 4½"(23cm x 11cm) loaf tin with bakewell paper and sit in a tray of ice and some water.
Pour in some liquid and place in segments and some peel. Allow to set slightly before using remaining segments, peel and liquid to build up layers.
When firm, turn out and slice using an electric knife. Serve with a little cointreau-flavoured whipped cream. (Betty Allen)

MULLED WINE

Mulled wine and mince pies are the classic Christmas welcome. You can make the spicy syrup and strain it and keep it, heating it and adding wine as required.

6 large oranges
8oz(225g) sugar
1 tablespoon whole cloves
2 cinnamon sticks
1 teaspoon ground nutmeg
3 pints(1.7 litres) water
2 bottles of red wine

Roughly cut the oranges and put into a large pan with the water, the sugar and the spices. Bring to the boil, stirring until the sugar has dissolved, and simmer gently for about half an hour. When required, bring the syrup to the boil and add the wine. Warm, but do not allow to boil again. Ladle into warmed glasses.
(Kirsty Burrell)

WHITE WINE REFRESHER

An ideal drink for summer parties. Slice 3 oranges, 2 lemons and half a cucumber into a big glass bowl. Add 5fl oz(150ml) orange liqueur and leave to macerate for half an hour. Add 3 bottles of chilled dry white wine (Muscadet is good) and 1½ bottles of soda water, then ice and borage or mint leaves, and perhaps a few sliced strawberries or raspberries.
(Kirsty Burrell)

BIRCH SAP WINE

1 gallon freshly collected birch sap (it does not keep)
1lb(450g) raisins
2lb(900g) sugar
juice of 2 lemons
1oz(25g) general purpose wine-making yeast

Boil the sap, sugar and raisins for 15-20 minutes then pour into a bucket, add the lemon juice and leave to cool to blood heat. Add the yeast, and leave to ferment in the covered bucket for three to five days. Strain into a one gallon demi john and seal with an air lock. Leave in a warm place until fermentation ceases, then strain and bottle. Allow to mature for at least a month.
(Tess Darwin)

ROSEHIP SYRUP

This recipe, recommended during the last war for its high vitamin C content, can be diluted to drink or poured over desserts.

2lb(900g) rosehips
3 pints(1.7 litres) boiling water
1lb(450g) sugar

Remove stalks and wash the rosehips, then chop them finely (this is most easily done in a liquidiser) and place immediately in the boiling water (any delay after chopping will diminish the vitamin C content). Leave away from the heat to infuse for 15 minutes, then strain through a jelly bag. Return the contents of the bag to the pan and add another 1½ pints(900ml) boiling water. Leave to infuse for 10 minutes, then strain again. Put all the juice in a clean saucepan and boil down until about 1½ pints(900ml) is left, then add the sugar and boil for another 5 minutes. Pour into sterile bottles and seal. The syrup should keep for several months, but use bottles within a week after opening.
(Tess Darwin)

SLOE GIN

An unusual, slightly astringent liqueur, ideal to serve at Christmas. It is reputed to keep for two or three years, but I have never been able to test that!

8oz(225g) sloes
8oz(225g) sugar
5 blanched almonds
1 bottle gin

Wash the sloes and prick with a fork. Half fill a kilner jar with the fruit, add the almonds and top up with gin. Leave in a fairly warm place for at least 2 to 3 months, shaking occasionally, then bottle, either strained or with the sloes still in.
(Tess Darwin)

ELDERBERRY CORDIAL

A very old recipe for a remedy against winter coughs and colds, to be drunk diluted in hot or cold water. It can also be added to red wine for a delicious hot punch.

3lb(1.4kg) elderberries
2lb(900g) sugar (approx)
whole cloves

Wash the elderberries and remove their stalks. Cover with water and simmer until very soft. Strain through a jelly bag or muslin cloth, collecting the juice in a measuring jug. Add 1lb(450g) sugar and 12 cloves to each pint of juice, and simmer gently for 15-20 minutes. Strain and bottle when cold.
(Tess Darwin)

SORREL SAUCE

This appetising clear green sauce with a sharp flavour is an excellent accompaniment to fish and egg dishes.

8oz(225g) sorrel leaves
1oz(25g) butter
1oz(25g) flour
5fl oz(150ml) stock
chives or parsley

Finely chop the sorrel leaves and simmer for 5 minutes, then drain, retaining the cooking water to add to the stock. Melt the butter, return the sorrel to the pan and stir in the flour over a low heat. Carefully add the stock to make a clear, fairly thin sauce. Liquidise if necessary. Serve garnished with fresh chopped chives or parsley.
(Tess Darwin)

ONION MARMALADE

1lb(450g) thinly sliced onions
1 teaspoon soft brown sugar
1½ dessertspoons white wine vinegar
2oz(50g) butter

Melt butter in a thick bottomed pan. Cook onions and sugar, covered, until soft. Add vinegar and cook uncovered until reduced. Season before serving.

ROWAN JELLY

3lb(1.4kg) rowan berries
2lb(900g) sugar (approx)
2 pints(1.2 litres) water
3 tablespoons lemon juice

Wash the berries and remove their stalks. Simmer in the water and lemon juice until soft. Pour the contents of the pan into a jelly bag and leave overnight, collecting the juice in a measuring jug. Add 1lb(450g) sugar to each pint of juice, and boil until set. Pour into jars and seal. (Tess Darwin)

WHOLE ORANGE MARMALADE

The easiest way to make marmalade.

3lb(1.4kg)Seville oranges
6 lemons
6 pints(3.4 litres) water
6lb(2.7kg) sugar

Scrub the fruit and put into a pan with the water. Simmer until the skin is soft (about 1½ hours). Take out the fruit. Leave the water in the pan. Cut the oranges into small chunks. Liquidise the lemons. Tie the pips in a piece of muslin and hang them from the handle of the pan so that they dangle in to the pan and add the warmed sugar. Stir over heat until the sugar has dissolved, then bring to a rolling boil and sustain until setting point is reached (a blob will wrinkle on a saucer cooled in the freezer). Leave to settle for 15 minutes, stir and pot in warmed jars.
(Kirsty Burrell)

LEMON CURD

Home made lemon curd is completely different from the lurid gelatinous substance the supermarkets stock. It keeps for 3 months in the fridge, longer in the freezer.

grated rind and juice of 2 large lemons
3oz(75g) butter
7oz(200g) sugar
3 eggs

Put butter, sugar, lemon juice and rind into the top of a double boiler, with water simmering underneath, and stir until dissolved. Take the pan off the heat and stir in the beaten eggs. Return to the heat and cook very slowly until the mixture thickens. Do not let it boil. Put into small jars or yogurt or cream cartons for freezing.
(Kirsty Burrell)

DELICATE GREEN SAUCE

Herbs for green sauces are flexible. Don't be afraid to use what you have to hand, balancing out the flavours. For a quick sauce, delicious with fried fish, simply whizz a bunch of watercress and a carton of yogurt together in the food processor. A bunch of minced parsley (preferably the flat-leaved kind) stirred into a *béchamel* sauce is excellent with poached chicken, eggs or fish.

8-10 leaves spinach
8 sprigs watercress
4 sprigs tarragon
4 sprigs parsley
½ pint(300ml) mayonnaise

Blanch the herbs for 2 minutes in boiling water, drain and squeeze dry and liquidise with a little of the mayonnaise. Mix with the rest of the mayonnaise just before serving. This is the perfect accompaniment for cold salmon. For a hot green sauce add the herb mixture to a hollandaise sauce. (Kirsty Burrell)

HERB APPLE JELLY

Herb apple jellies are excellent accompaniments to hot or cold roast meats. Crab apples or under-ripe wind-falls are ideal.

6lb(2.7kg) apples
2 pints(1.2 litres) water
1 large bunch of herbs (mint or rosemary for lamb, sage for pork etc)
1 pint(600ml) cider vinegar
1lb(450g) sugar for every pint of liquid
fresh leaves of whichever herb is used

Chop the apples roughly and simmer them till soft in the water with the bunch of herbs. Add vinegar and boil gently for 10 minutes. Strain overnight through a jelly bag. For every pint of juice add 1lb(450g) sugar. Dissolve over a gentle heat, then bring to a rolling boil and sustain until setting point is reached (a blob of jelly will wrinkle on a saucer cooled in the freezer). Skim, add fresh herb leaves and allow to cool slightly before potting. (Kirsty Burrell)

SPICED PLUMS

3lb(1.4kg) plums
1lb(450g) sugar
½ pint(300ml) cider vinegar
1 blade mace
2"(5cm) stick cinnamon
1 teaspoon whole cloves
10 allspice berries
2 small red chillis (dried)

In a heavy-based pan stir together the sugar and the vinegar until the sugar has dissolved. Add the spices and simmer gently for five minutes. Put the plums into a blanching basket and lower them into the pan. Cook until the plums are just tender, but not falling to pieces. Drain the plums. Boil down the liquid until syrupy. Pack the fruit into warm, dry kilner jars and strain the syrup over them, making sure all the plums are covered. If you make them in autumn they will be ready for Christmas. (Kirsty Burrell)

126

Index